I have always been fascinated by Africa. The excitement and danger of wild animals. The exotic tribes and their customs. The mystery and majestic beauty of the landscape.

Then I had the opportunity to travel to Africa and later to India and China.

Diary of a Wildlife Photographer is a record of some of my adventures.

Jan Latta

Diary of a WILDLIFE PHOTOGRAPHER

Jan Latta

ABC Books

Come on a great adventure

...with me—

Contents

4 AFRICA CALLING

22 GORILLAS AND GUERILLAS

28 CHIMPS AND CHEETAHS

36 FLYING OVER AFRICA

44 THE MAGIC OF AFRICA

56 FOLLOWING THE ELEPHANTS

78 LIONS AND LUXURY

84 CUDDLING CHIMPS

92 TIGERS AND TARA

102 PLAYING WITH PANDAS

CHAPTER ONE

Africa calling

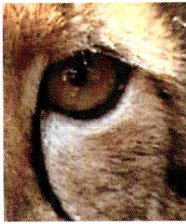

My fascination with Africa starts when I see Karl Ammann's African wildlife photography. His images are mesmerising. I decide to fly to Africa to meet Karl and design a photo essay on his work. I book my flight, but then start to wonder if it is safe to travel alone. I ask my friend Jon to come with me so that I have a travelling companion.

We arrive at Nairobi, the capital city of Kenya, after a long and tiring flight. The city is choked with pollution. There is traffic chaos everywhere. Impatient drivers are honking horns. Hundreds of people are walking in between cars, creating more traffic problems.

Finally we reach the cool comfort of the Muthaiga Club, and I'm very grateful Karl has booked us rooms. This private club has a grand history of adventurers who have stayed here. Karen Blixen and Denys Finch Hatton, on whom the film *Out of Africa* is based, had cocktails here. Beryl Markham, the famous pilot who wrote *West with the Night,* told her adventure stories here.

I call Karl and he invites us to go to his home and meet his wife Kathy. I am sitting in the garden sipping tea when I notice a cheetah sauntering across the lawn. I feel

a bit foolish saying, 'There's a cheetah in your garden,' so I wait breathlessly for something to happen. Karl sees the cheetah and gets up to stroke him affectionately. He invites me to do the same. It is amazing to be close to this magnificent animal. His name is Moto. I nervously pat his head, feel the wiry fur on top, and the smoother fur on his rump. Karl puts his fingers into Moto's mouth and I hear a deep, contented purr.

Karl and Kathy talk about some of the tented camps we might enjoy. I ask what it is like living in a tent. Kathy says, 'Some tents are pegged into the earth and are temporary, while others are permanent and have modern bathroom plumbing.' In fact, they lived in a tent for years when Karl was developing Intrepids Camp in the Maasai Mara. Karl has made reservations for us at some of these camps, but suggests we go to Treetops Hotel first.

Moto in the garden.

▲ *My tented camps.*

A herd of elephants on the move.

Treetops

We hire a driver and leave the next morning for our first adventure. Treetops is in the Aberdare National Park and is a famous tourist attraction. In 1952, Princess Elizabeth climbed up the wooden staircase at Treetops. She went up a princess and came down a queen – her father, King George VI, had died during the night. She became Queen Elizabeth II.

Treetops is a hotel literally built in the trees. I climb up the rambling wooden structure and venture into my tiny room. It's rather rustic, but great fun for my first night.

I hear someone yell, 'Elephants!' and I clamber up to the lookout platform. Twelve elephants lumber past. What beautiful prehistoric mud sculptures they are! They have come to dig for salt. After eating the nourishing salt they drink litres of water, then squirt it over their bodies. They are very affectionate, nuzzling each other with their trunks and making soft rumbling noises. The little calves trot along beside their mothers. It's amazing they don't get tangled up in their mother's legs.

Elephants outside Treetops.

A calf stays close to its mother.

7

It's getting dark and the spotlights are turned on. The elephants have turned a golden brown in the light and I watch their slow-moving shapes glide past.

Next stop is an overnight stay at Outspan Hotel near Nyeri in the central highlands. My room is magnificent and looks out onto a beautiful garden. To complete the scene, elegant peacocks are strutting past. I meet Jon for a drink and hear a funny scratching sound. I turn around to see the peacocks tip-toeing into the bar area. They slip and slide on the highly polished wooden floor, landing in a flurry of exotic feathers. It's a comical contrast to the very colonial English setting.

My first game drive

My first game drive is one I'll never forget. As we drive along a dirt track in our jeep, I see fresh mounds of steaming wet elephant dung. I know a large elephant is

Peacocks strut around the dining room at the Outspan Hotel.

Elephants charge the jeep.

Exotic golden crested cranes.

Tiny timid dik-dik.

The beautiful striped bongo.

very close. We drive around a bend that has high bushes on either side, then I see him.

He is huge and he doesn't want us on his path. He is protecting six females. Two are startled and amble off, but two are still in front of the jeep and two are behind us. The females start running. Elephant bums wobbling on the run is a rather funny sight – but our situation isn't funny. The bull elephant is flapping his ears, screaming and trumpeting and terrorising the wits out of me. It's just a 'mock' charge, but it feels very real to me. The bull disappears into the bush and I relax, then out he comes again, charging down the path after us. I've never been so breathless with fright.

Nanyuki

Back to the comfort of the hotel and I relive the day's adventure around the fire. Next morning, a driver takes us to the Mount Kenya Safari Club in Nanyuki. Without any ceremony, we pass the equator on the way. The Mount Kenya Safari Club was started many years ago by the film star William Holden. It is very English country mansion in style, with exotic birds strutting around the beautiful manicured lawns.

I go to the animal orphanage adjacent to the Safari Club to see some of the animals I may not see in the wild. I love the tiny delicate dik-dik – a deer-like animal less than a metre high, and very shy. To find dik-diks in the bush, you have to look for a little circle of their poo pellets, because they always use the same area to go to the toilet.

I tap the shell of a 100-year-old turtle and play with an elusive bush baby. This tiny monkey sits in the cup of

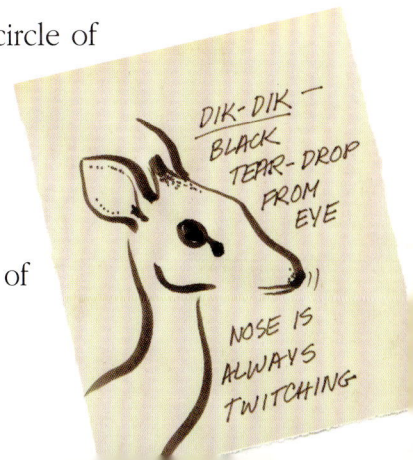
DIK-DIK —
BLACK
TEAR-DROP
FROM
EYE

NOSE IS
ALWAYS
TWITCHING

The pigmy hippo.

my hand. He has huge eyes and can leap up to two metres. I try to get close to the rare bongo (a type of antelope) to photograph his beautiful pattern of tan stripes, but he's too timid. I get very close to a pygmy hippo, the camera almost inside his open mouth, then *wham!* I get knocked over. At first I think an animal has run into me, then I realise I've been electrocuted on the security fence. Dazed, I walk back to the Safari Club.

Samburu

Now it's safari time. The word 'safari' appropriately means journey in Swahili. Another dusty jeep ride, this time to Larsens Camp in Samburu, situated on the Uaso Nyiro River. At the camp, I have a small tent just a few metres from the river. To enter, I unzip the tent flap and I must always remember to zip it back because naughty monkeys try to come into the tent. Inside is a bed and rough shelves for my clothes. At the back of the tent, there's a small shower, basin and toilet.

Next morning, my wake-up call is the sound of the tent being unzipped and tea and biscuits left on the table outside. A monkey jumps down from the tree and steals my biscuits in a flash. I'll have to be quicker tomorrow.

We drive out onto the plains and I have a swivel-head because I don't want to miss anything. We stop by a herd of impala – beautiful deer-like animals. They let out a warning bark and all faces point in the same direction. This means a predator is close. The impala leap high in the air, giving the predator the illusion they are bigger than they are. The driver circles around, trying to find the cause for the alarm. Then I see a magnificent leopard,

A bush baby.

My tent at Larsens Camp.

A mischievous monkey.

A young calf drinking mother's milk.

perfectly camouflaged in the grass. What a thrill! The leopard turns to look at me, then with a swish of its tail disappears into the tall grass.

We pass a herd of elephants. They are friendly this time, so the driver stops the jeep. I take hundreds of photographs and watch the elephants without fear. There is a tiny baby sucking on mother's milk and I notice that the mother's teat is tucked between her front legs. She has to move her leg forward so the baby can drink.

Maasai Mara

The driver takes us back to Wilson Airport in Nairobi, then we fly to Intrepids Camp in the Maasai Mara. The Maasai Mara is a magical place located near the south-west corner of Kenya and Tanzania. Karl has recommended a good driver, so I meet with him and discuss the next day's photography. The camp is great. My tent is on a wooden platform, the bush is all around me.

Staff wake me at 4.30 am and we drive out in the cold, dark morning. When it's light I see something

Impalas looking for the leopard hiding in the grass.

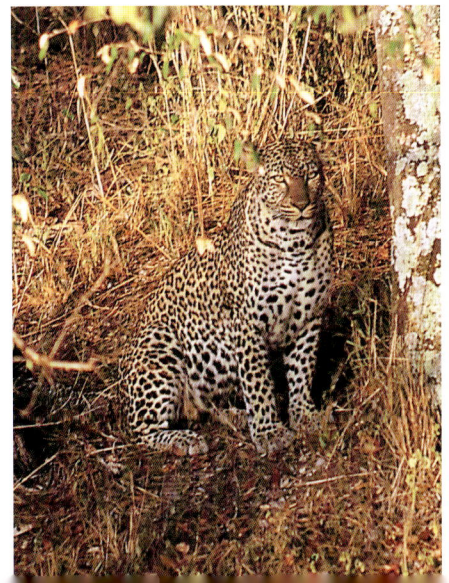

shimmering on the horizon. It's a herd of giraffe. They are majestic in the golden morning light and I try to capture them on film. I notice the Maasai giraffe has a different pattern to the Samburian giraffe. The tan patches are softer and spread out around the edges.

Hundreds of animals are scattered over the plains – buffalo, waterbuck, topi, Thompson's gazelle and impala. I ask the guide the difference between the gazelle and the impala, because they both look like a deer. He tells me to look at their rear ends. The impala has a marking on his bottom, and it looks like an 'M'.

It is fantastic to be in such a wide open space – 360 degrees of endless plains, the sky enormous, the landscape forever. One lonely tree marks the horizon. I feel so tiny in this magnificent savanna.

Out on the plains again after breakfast and I see the funny warthogs called the Kenya Express – so called because they run behind each other with their tails straight up in the air, looking like a train. They are very ugly up close. Some have huge, dangerous curved tusks which they use to dig for food, or to fight to the death.

I take a photograph of a mother rhinoceros with her baby, who is sucking noisily. The rhino has two tiny oxpecker (or tick-tick) birds on her back. They are very important to most of the African animals as they eat the ticks and bugs from the animals' skin. Later in the day I see a giraffe curl back its lips and a little tick-tick bird hops in and picks the giraffe's teeth. I watch through my binoculars, fascinated. I'm too far away to take a photograph. Pity!

The M on the impala's bottom distinguishes it from other deer.

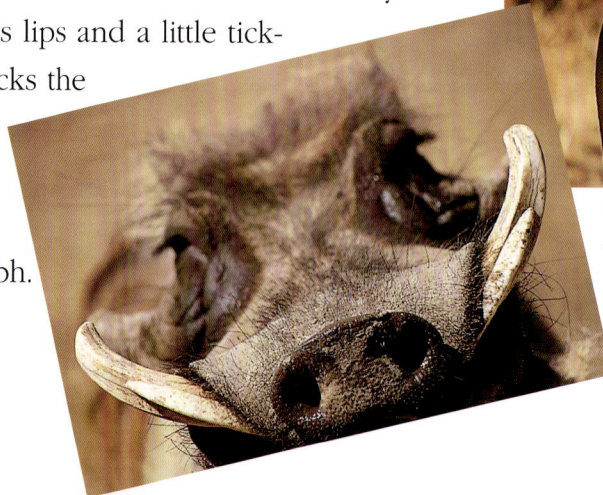

A warthog with dangerous tusks.

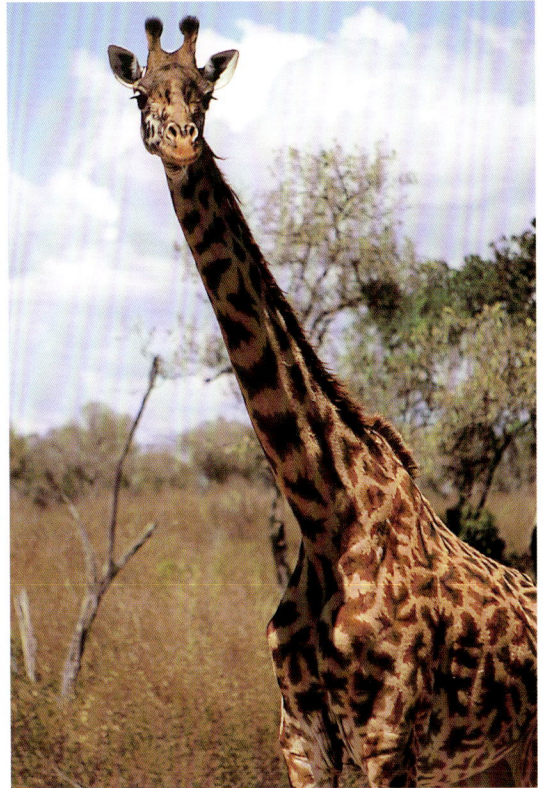

Different patterns on the Maasai giraffe (below) and the Samburian giraffe (left).

I bounce happily back to camp for a great dinner. Everything tastes better in the bush! After dinner I sit around the camp fire listening to stories told by a Maasai warrior. He is exotic, with colourful beads around his body, and a cloak to keep him warm. His earlobes are very long and decorated with beaded earrings. He has three spears propped up by the fire. He walks Jon and I back to our tents each night to protect us from wild animals. I wonder about the effect of a spear against a lion, but I'm told I'm safe. It's very cold at night and I'm delighted to discover a hot water bottle tucked into my bed. Bliss.

I fall asleep to the sound of rain on the canvas roof, thinking I already have a lifetime of memories. In the night I hear the growl of a lion and it's dangerously close.

A Maasai warrior.

Rescuing the gazelle.

In the morning I see he's killed a zebra in the camp area. Much too close for comfort.

The next day we stop by a river and I get out of the jeep to take a photograph of hippos. I notice a large crocodile lazing by the bank. They always look asleep, but I know they can move with lightning speed when they want to attack. I try to concentrate on the hippos. They blow, snort, and make a strange grunting sound before they submerge themselves in the muddy water. Their tails wiggle frantically when they swish their dung

A lazy crocodile on the bank of the river.

out of the way, usually onto the next hippo. I'm close enough to smell them, but I can only detect a wet horse, stable smell. Not wanting to test my luck with the crocodile, I run back to the safety of the jeep.

Up ahead, I see something I can't identify lying on the ground and ask the driver to stop. It's a tiny Thompson's gazelle calling for its dead mother. It's cold and shivering. I ask the driver if I can take it back to camp. He's reluctant but I plead with him and he finally agrees. I remove the canvas seat cover from the jeep and put the gazelle inside it. I hold the baby close to me for warmth. Its tiny face looks up at me and it lets out a little bleat. On the way back to camp we pass two male lions and I'm a bit nervous because I'm holding 'lunch' in an open jeep.

Back at camp I place the baby gazelle by the kitchen

Male lions looking for lunch.

fire and put milk on my finger. It takes a while, but finally it sucks on my finger and I trickle milk down into its mouth. The next morning the gazelle is wobbling around on spindly legs, wagging its tail and looking happy. I hope it survives.

Today I ask the guide to search for a pride of lions. This is a challenge because lions haven't been seen in the area for days. After bumping across the plains for half an hour, he stops the jeep. He looks through his binoculars and says, 'Lions!'

'Where, where?' I impatiently ask.

'Over by the tree,' he replies.

But I can't see anything, just the swaying grass.

We slowly drive up to the pride. Sixteen lions emerge

The lions' eyes reflected in the headlights of the jeep.

The pride eats – and the vultures wait for left-overs.

The menacing buffalo.

from the tall grass. I'm breathless with excitement. A huge male is only a metre away…can he jump into the open jeep? Is it safe? He lazily watches me with his tawny eyes then saunters off to join the pride. The female lions settle down in the grass and I watch the little cubs frolicking and playing with each other. We stay until dusk so I can take a photograph of the pride with their eyes reflected in the headlights of the jeep. Now it's dangerous. It's night, the lions are growling, and I'm in an open jeep. We drive back to the safety of our camp and our tents.

Now I've photographed the 'big five'. Elephant, buffalo, leopard, lions and rhino.

I see the pride again the next morning, with a kill. A topi. The males eat first, then the females, the cubs last. The tiny cubs are always trying to sneak in for their share and their mothers scold them with snarls. The males finally strut off, their bellies bulging. The females and cubs finish eating. The ugly scavenging hyenas will eat the left-overs. They circle the lions, waiting their turn. The vultures hover for their share.

Next day I visit a Maasai village. The Maasai people

Colourful beads adorn the Maasai.

are nomads, which means they move around from place to place. When they make their home they build round huts made of cow dung and mud. They drink a mixture of milk and blood from their sacred cows. I'm invited into a Maasai mud hut. It's pitch black, smoky and suffocating. There is a very old, wizened woman sitting in the corner. When I go outside I gulp a mouthful of fresh air. But the smell of wet dung around the hut is not pleasant.

Some of the Maasai women are exquisitely beautiful, with fine long necks and graceful postures. The men are very handsome. They wear exotic beads around their limbs and tiny plaited ribbons of hair cascade down their back. The children, after a shy pause, hassle me for treats.

On the last morning I see the pride of lions again, lazing in the sun. They look up when we approach, then flop down to continue snoozing. We drive off to leave them in peace. The jeep coughs to a stop and won't start again. Buffalo are moving towards us and we are stranded in the middle of a herd. I'm nervous, but at least I get some good photographs. The buffalo stand and look at me in the most menacing way. Another jeep comes along, we explain our car troubles, and they go for help.

The buffalo stop eyeballing me and help finally arrives.

A Maasai herdsman and his mud hut.

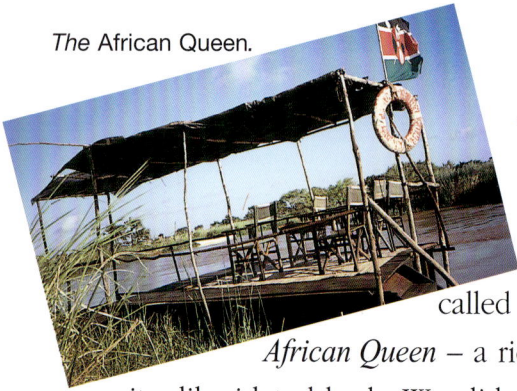

Tana River

Karl suggests we visit a new camp run by a naturalist called Renaldo Retief. We board the *African Queen* – a rickety boat, aptly named for its dilapidated look. We glide down the river for four hours – past village life, huge mango trees and exotic birds. The camp is situated near Kipini, where the Tana River empties into the Indian Ocean. Only two other guests are at the camp, plus Renaldo, a cook and the camp helpers.

My tent is erected. The shower unit and toilet are by the side of my tent. The toilet is just a hole in the ground with hessian pegged around it for privacy. I try the outdoor novelty, but it collapses and falls on top of me. I'm so embarrassed. I try my luck with the shower. This is a bucket with holes in the bottom, suspended from a tree. The wind is so strong that the water goes everywhere except on my body. I give up and go to bed.

My tent is tiny, with a camp bed constructed of canvas stretched across wooden legs. I have pegs to keep my clothes off the ground and a torch by my bed. I zip up my tent and go to sleep with the sound of the bush around me.

Next morning we all climb into a canoe and paddle up the river. I see crocodiles lazing on the muddy river banks. Then the river gets very narrow and shallow. We paddle round a bend and are confronted by a pod of snorting hippos. Our guide says, 'This could be dangerous, there could be a mock charge.'

'Oh, do we show mock fear?' replies my friend.

The tide is going out and it's very dangerous. It seems to take forever to pass the hippos. I nervously take

Hippos in the shallow river.

SAND DOLLAR SHELL

TWO SLIT HOLES IN THIS VERY THIN SHELL

photographs but I'm shaking so much I'm not sure if I'm in focus.

I walk along the safety of the beach and collect fragile 'sand dollars' – beautiful, fine shells that I collect for friends. It feels strange to walk on a beach in Africa, sharing it with wild animals instead of bathers. Walking back to camp I notice a lone hippo in the water, twitching his ears.

My guide has told me that the mud around the river has the finest texture and it makes a perfect 'mud' bath.

Excited about a beauty treatment, I put on my swim-suit and go down to the edge of the lake. The mud is very squelchy between my toes and I cautiously slide into the water. I cover myself with the fine mud, even my face and hair. Then I notice the hippo is getting close. I search for a tree to climb, just in case. The mud starts to set but I won't go back into the water with the hippo. I crunch my way back to my tent with bits of caked-on mud falling off me. After many buckets of water my hair is squeaky clean and my skin feels great.

Lamu Island

We leave camp early the next morning in a motor boat to get through the low tides. A crocodile slides under the boat and I look to see if the blades have cut him in half. Two men have to push us the last few metres and then we have a frantic jeep ride to catch the plane.

Our plane lands at Lamu Island, one of the oldest towns on Kenya's northern coast. I stay overnight at a friend's house – it's next to a mosque and I'm woken by the Muslim call to prayer. The loudspeakers make sure everyone hears the call.

My friend's house at Lamu.

I move to Peponi Hotel the next day and my room is fabulous – right on the water with the sea lapping on three sides. I have a great four-poster bed, billowing net curtains and the temperature controlled by opening or closing the shutters. This is a very different Africa, the people a mix of the Arab and Persian traders who settled here.

Another flight in a tiny plane and I sit next to a black-robed woman who must be scared of flying because she prays all the way to Malindi. We catch the train back to Nairobi and stay again at the Muthaiga Club.

Mzee

Karl collects us the next morning. Kathy is waiting at their front door, holding the ugliest chimp I have ever seen. The sun is shining through his pink ears and he has an impish look on his face. He holds out his arms for a hug and climbs into my arms. He is cheeky, naughty and utterly adorable. His name is Mzee, which means old man. I'm besotted! He climbs down, then holds my hand to show me around the house, often going under low tables, where I follow. I want to play with him forever.

Mzee.

Karl and Kathy found Mzee when they were in the Congo. They saw a lot of 'bush meat' being sold. That means primates (gorillas, chimps, bonobos) that have been killed, smoked, then sold to eat. When they saw a tiny little scrawny chimp with the face of an old man looking up at them pathetically, Kathy and Karl decided to rescue him. When they returned to Kenya they had to get permission to keep him, and when that was granted, Karl decided to start a chimp sanctuary. The famous primologist, Jane Goodall, later became involved in setting up the Sweetwater Chimp Sanctuary, about an hour from Nanyuki.

Mzee and Kathy.

Marabou storks resting on a tree.

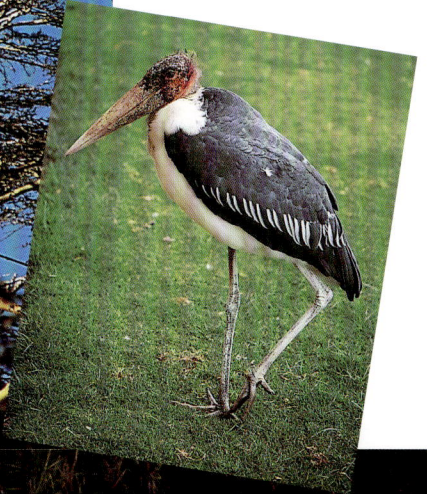

Next day Karl and Kathy invite us to Lake Naivashi. They hire a flat-bottom boat and we glide through the reeds onto the lake. Beautiful birds are everywhere – cranes delicately tip-toeing through the grass looking for insects, storks looking like old judges, huge pelicans, and fabulous fish eagles soaring high in the air hunting for prey. We nudge up to a small island on the lake for our picnic lunch.

Our adventure starts when we motor back. Hippos surface close to the boat, reminding me of oily submarines, then submerge again. It's frightening because I don't know when they'll surface again, or how close to the boat. Then the engine stalls. The rudder has caught in a fishing net and we drift dangerously close to the hippos. Finally, Karl gets the motor started and we arrive back safely. We walk up to the jeep, only to discover it has two flat tyres.

We fly back home to Hong Kong. It's been a wonderful journey – seeing wild animals for the first time, touching a cheetah, playing with a chimp, and discovering the great beauty of Africa.

White and saddle bill storks.

gorillas and guerillas

After Jon and I return to Hong Kong I can't wait to plan the next trip. But my destination is very dangerous. Rwanda in East-Central Africa. I want to photograph the gorillas there. Again Karl comes to the rescue, making inquiries about my safety.

I receive a fax from the travel agent at the gorilla booking office in Rwanda, and it reads, 'The rebels are attacking at 25 km from Kinigi Gorilla Office, that's the reason no car is allowed to go there except tourist, because it's in a battlefield. The tourists are safe because they are protected by the army in that area.'

Jon and I decide to take the risk. The rumblings of war seem to be another local dispute between the Tutsi and the Hutu tribes. We fly to Kigali, the capital of Rwanda, and the travel agent meets us. He gives Jon the keys to the car and says, 'Go that way, over the mountains.'

I say, 'No, we don't know the way, we need a driver.'

After a lot of negotiating, a driver is assigned to us and we start our steep climb. This becomes very dangerous because our driver won't stay on the right side of the road. The mountain bends are suicidal – and there is a sheer

A baby gorilla peeps over the bushes at me.

drop to the bottom. I let out a yelp and beg the driver to please drive on the right side of the road. He shrugs, grins and drives correctly. Now I can admire the view without thinking I am going to have a head-on collision.

The scenery looks like Switzerland, with the same pointy shaped-mountains, the valley sprinkled with millions of multi-coloured flowers.

The beautiful scenery is contrasted by the military road-blocks. I'm very nervous. The car is stopped often, my passport is taken and inspected. Finally, the driver stops at our destination. A grim-looking building, once used as army barracks, has had a coat of paint and is now called guest quarters. I ask for some water and make the mistake of seeing where it comes from – it's stored in a rusty bath tub in the kitchen. The kitchen has not been cleaned for a long time.

Gunfire breaks the silence of the night and I sit up in fear.

Next morning, Jon and I meet our guide for the gorilla trek. He tells us the rules. Never make eye contact with a gorilla – it's threatening. Move slowly – no sudden movements. If a gorilla approaches – get into a submissive pose.

The big silverback (above) and a young gorilla.

And up the mountain I trudge. It's a tough climb. For over two hours I struggle up the slippery slopes. Sometimes I have to crawl across a tangle of vines with no ground underneath. I try not to look down.

The guide finally stops. Breathlessly I wait and listen. He makes a series of grunts to let the gorillas know we are here. Then slowly I move forward.

A little gorilla peeps over the vines at me. It is a glorious moment. Then I see the mother, and later the family group and the leader – the big silverback. He's called a silverback because he has white hair down his back. The silverback is looking at me and I can't help it, I look back at him. I know I've been told not to, but his dark eyes are mesmerising. Finally I lower my eyes and get into submissive pose. I slowly lift my head again. He's still looking at me and, for another moment, I enjoy eye contact with a rare, endangered mountain gorilla.

The silverback starts to walk into the forest and I follow. Suddenly there is no silverback, and no guide. I am in a bamboo forest, alone. The forest closes in on me. I nervously squeak out a few 'hellos' and the guide comes back to rescue me.

A female gorilla walks purposefully towards me. I back up to a large rock and crouch down. She brushes past me to sit on the rock above my head. I nervously look up behind me to see she is lying back, picking her teeth. She looks so relaxed, I start to relax too.

There is a gentle thumping sound and I see two young gorillas playing in the vines. The young male is play-acting, thumping his chest. I don't know how loud that sound can be until the big silverback lets out his blood-curdling roar. I'm frozen to the spot. The guide says he is only showing his dominance and not to worry.

Mother and baby.

Having a sleep after eating.

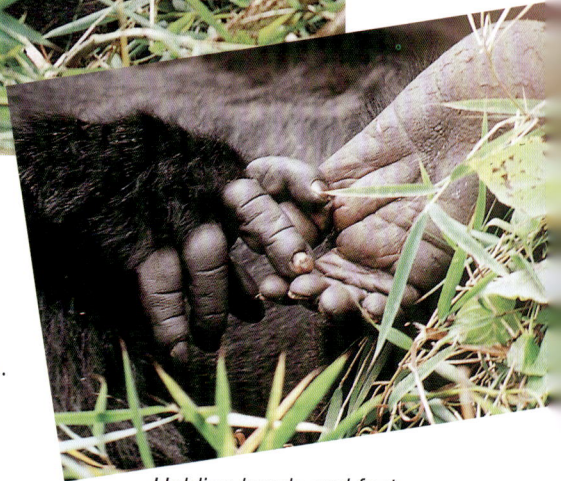

Holding hands and feet.

The hour goes so quickly and I am soon struggling back down the mountain.

The next day our guide takes us to a different location. The climb is steeper than yesterday. Although my lungs seem to be adjusting to the high altitude, I hire a 'pusher' and a 'puller' to help me up the mountain. One young man is in front of me holding onto my hand, the other at my back, pushing me up the steep slope. It's a torturous climb and I'm exhausted, but I want to see the gorillas again.

The gorillas are out in the open today, instead of in the jungle. The group is feeding and it's interesting to see the different types of plants and leaves they are eating. One gorilla is happily munching on leaves that have sharp thorns on the ends. He doesn't seem to mind. After his 'lunch' he has a nap. In the evening, gorillas make a nest by pulling down branches and leaves. They climb inside

A gorilla munches on leaves with sharp thorns.

their 'bed' and curl up to sleep. The next morning the silverback leads the family to a new location in the jungle.

On the climb back down the mountain my guide tells me there are fewer than 600 mountain gorillas left in the world. I'm stunned. These beautiful, gentle animals are so endangered. I decide to publish a book about the mountain gorillas. This is the start of *True to Life* books, photographic stories that help children understand endangered animals.

Driving back to Kigali is not pleasant. Road-blocks. Security checks. Passports examined. We give a soldier a lift and I feel very nervous until he gets out. It's a very odd feeling to be a tourist in the middle of a civil war. Our fax said the military would protect us but, so far, they have not been friendly.

There is talk about a demonstration in the city and I can't wait to leave. When we fly out, I don't relax until Kigali is a tiny dot on the landscape. We land safely in Nairobi and drive to Nanyuki. After getting lost a few times we finally arrive to celebrate New Year's Eve with Karl and Kathy.

Having a good scratch.

My guides who help me up the mountain.

CHAPTER THREE

Chimps and cheetahs

Karl and Kathy have built a new house in Nanyuki, near Mount Kenya, and I have been invited to stay with them. The house is set in a wonderful rambling garden with Mount Kenya a dramatic backdrop. Mzee comes running out to greet me in his boisterous way, scrambling straight up my body for a great hug.

The next morning I walk out onto the veranda to have breakfast and Moto, the cheetah, is relaxing next to the table. It is great to see him again. I try to get close to take a photograph, but he snarls at me and I have to retreat. I was lucky the first time when he let me pat him. Disappointed, I try instead to take a photograph of a tiny monkey. This is impossible because he keeps sitting on my head. I try to entice him with milk and fruit, but my head is his favourite destination. He also likes peeing down the back of my jumper.

Mzee giving me a kiss.

After changing my clothes we all prepare for a picnic with Mzee. I climb into the jeep and make the mistake of sitting on his side of the seat. He bites my hand. Kathy scolds him and twists his ears, then puts him on the other side of her. During the journey Mzee looks across at me,

then very gently reaches over and holds my hand. He understands he hurt me and it's his way of saying sorry.

Our picnic spot is on the top of a hill with a magnificent view across the plains. Mzee takes my hand again and we explore the area together. He climbs up a tree and looks puzzled when I don't follow him. Then he takes his favourite fizzy drink and slurps it down. Kathy tells me that at home he goes to the fridge, gets his drink, takes off the lid and, after drinking it, puts the empty bottle in the bin. He also shares his drink with a three-year-old boy. They're good friends!

After the picnic, we drive to an area where Karl knows there is a rhino I can get close to. He stops the jeep and says, 'No sudden movements, do everything very slowly.'

I get out of the jeep, expecting to see the rhino in the distance. But he is lying in the grass just a metre away. He stands up and ambles off and I follow, taking photographs. He is massive, but strangely beautiful with his deep folds of mud-covered flesh. I photograph every crevice and fold on his prehistoric body.

Rhinos have very poor eyesight, so they charge at anything that moves. The trick is to move very, very slowly. Finally, I think it safe to go up to him and touch his horn.

It is interesting to see the difference between the black and white rhinos of Africa. The black has a pointy mouth and the white has a square-shaped mouth. Both are mud coloured, something they love wallowing in.

Mzee up a tree at the picnic.

Sharing a drink with his friend.

I get close enough to touch the rhino's horn.

Rhinos having a fight.

The rhino ambles over to a lovely muddy area and I take photographs of him rolling in the mud.

We drive along the dirt road and I see three rhinos, plump and posing under a tree. But this trio is not friendly. I get out to take photographs of two rhinos having a fight, but keep the jeep close behind. I have a few frantic runs back to the safety of the jeep.

Later, a rhino uses the spare tyre of the jeep as a scratching post and the jeep rocks back and forth from the strength of his horn.

Next, we visit a large property owned by Windenstein Ol Joji. This generous man has a full-time vet living on his property and any orphaned animals are looked after until they can be released back into the bush. We look in at the orphans: an oryx – a type of antelope – head-butts Karl, wanting to be too friendly with his long sharp horns; a tawny eagle recovering from a damaged wing; and a

Black and white rhinos. You can see the difference in the shape of their mouths.

Enjoying a mud bath.

Owl and tawny eagle.

An ostrich digesting grass.

beautiful tiny owl with pink eyelids.

I start taking photographs of an ostrich that is pecking away at the grass. After a few minutes I notice a large lump appear on his throat. It slowly goes down his long neck, being digested along the way. It has a fascinating face, with eyes almost on the side of its head, and two cute tufts of feathers that look like ears.

We all go for a walk, but I lag behind to change film. Out of the corner of my eye I see a cheetah running towards me. I don't know what to do. For some reason I'm not frightened. To see a cheetah running is such a magnificent sight. I look back and Karl motions me to kneel down. I think, *I'm level with its jaws now!* But I stay calm. The cheetah walks up to me, sniffs me, then flops down beside me. I have never experienced such a glorious moment.

We drive back and I'm in a state of bliss. I will never forget this day. I have had breakfast with a cheetah, a picnic with a chimp, and been sniffed by a wild cheetah!

Next day, Karl drives me to Intrepids Lodge, located

A cheetah a few metres away from me.

Elephants in the river and very close to my jeep.

near the Talek River, in Samburu. I see a mother elephant with her tiny calf separated from the herd. This is dangerous for the baby as the herd is not around for protection. Karl drives further down the track and I see the rest of the herd. Suddenly, a lion jumps over a log to attack a baboon and ends up in the middle of the elephants. The elephants start bellowing and charge the jeep, but Karl quickly backs away to a safe area. The lion has run around to my side of the jeep and comes towards my open window. I'm so intent on taking a photograph it doesn't occur to me to be frightened.

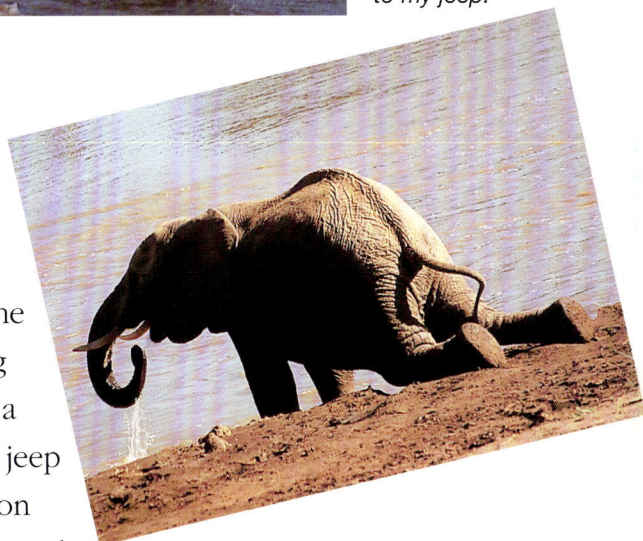

The herd calms down and I spend an hour taking photographs by the river. The elephants walk past the jeep in slow motion, just metres away. It's fascinating to see their long, coarse eyelashes and the texture of their skin. They amble past in silence, their huge padded feet cushioning the sound. The only noise I hear is their stomachs rumbling and the soft *swoosh* of air from their trunks. Two young male elephants, called bulls, are having a fight by the river. This is not a serious fight, but practice for testing their strength for the battles to come. After the tussle they cool off by fanning their ears.

Egret birds waiting for worms. Oxpecker birds pick bugs from the buffalo's nose.

I decide to focus on birds for a while. Egrets ride on the backs of buffaloes, performing the duties of tick-and-bug collectors. They also ride with elephants. When an elephant kicks a tuft of grass with its foot, it unearths nice juicy worms for the egret. It's fascinating watching the tiny egret stand so close to the enormous elephant's foot and not be trampled.

Back at the house in Nanyuki, I hear loud yelping near the garden. I rush out to see Mzee with Karl and Kathy's tiny Jack Russell, Rex, up a tree. Mzee has climbed up the tree holding Rex, who has the silliest look on his face. With the promise of a banana, Mzee is finally persuaded to bring Rex down.

Karl takes me to see Charlie, a new chimp he has been asked to look after. He was badly treated by his previous owner, so Karl has made a sanctuary for him on his property. Karl isn't sure how Charlie will react to me, so he goes into the enclosure first and I follow. Charlie

Mzee and Rex having fun together.

Playing with Charlie's lip.

Charlie grooms me and Mzee watches.

swoops into my arms with such force he nearly knocks me over. I stagger around until I find a tree stump to sit on. He starts to groom me, gently touching my face, nibbling on the hairs on my arm, playing with my watch. It is incredible looking into his intelligent eyes. He loves having his bottom lip wobbled and sticks out his tongue in bliss.

Next morning there's a great surprise – a cheetah cub up a tree in the garden. She is the latest addition to the Ammann 'family'. Her name is Charlotte. She trots inside and makes herself at home, sitting on the sofa and generally being inquisitive about her new abode. She is so affectionate and lets me get very close to her. I discover she loves beer. She puts her face into the beer and licks up the froth. She looks very funny with froth all over her nose.

After I fly back to Hong Kong I hear sad news about Moto. He has died. Each day he eats huge amounts of meat, and one day he eats a piece that has a bullet lodged inside. Nobody knew until it was too late.

Charlotte relaxes after climbing trees.

CHAPTER FOUR

Flying over Africa

I meet Roland Purcell when I am living in Hong Kong. He has set up the Mahale tented camp, by Lake Tanganyika in Tanzania, East Africa. The good news for me is that he has just bought a four-seater Cessna plane. These small bush planes can land on a dirt or grassy airstrip and go to places that are not easily accessible by land. This is exciting! I ask him if he will be my pilot and he agrees. After many hours of planning my next trip, we meet again in Kenya.

I climb into the tiny plane and we take off from Nairobi. We fly over the Rift Valley and Lake Turkana, famous for the thousands of flamingos that feed on the lake. When we approach, the area is a mass of pink. Thousands and thousands of flamingos take to the air when we fly over them. It's the most beautiful sight I have ever seen. I ask to go back again but Roland says no, it will frighten the birds.

We approach Lake Baringo. We circle above the dirt airstrip, searching for any animals on the strip, then we have a bumpy landing. I'm staying at the Ol Kokwa Island Camp in the middle of the lake. My tent is right on the lake front, my companions are a large green frog that

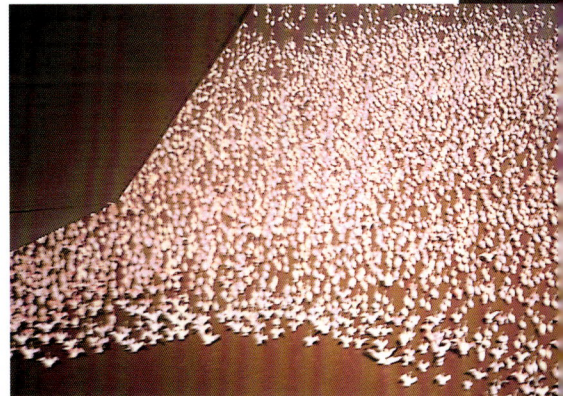

The view from my tent on Lake Baringo.

won't be persuaded to leave and two large spiders in the shower. The lake has perfect reflections.

Next morning, Roland is sitting outside his tent meditating with the sunrise. We get into a small canoe and paddle through the reeds. I'm a nervous wreck because hippos are everywhere. If they tip over our canoe the chances of survival are not good. I wonder why nature has given their ugly faces a continuous smile?

Roland lets me try flying the plane on the way back, but it is much harder than I thought. I hold the u-shaped 'steering wheel' and the plane goes *wobble, wobble*. Oops! I try to correct and the plane veers over to the right, then

Hippos and hundreds of birds on Lake Manyara.

to the left. Oops again. This is hard! With a grin, Roland takes the controls. He makes it look so easy.

We land at the East Tsavo National Park, one of the largest parks in Kenya. In the afternoon I cross the river to ride a camel. It is a nice tranquil ride except for the grunts and farts of my ill-tempered camel.

Tanzania

Then it's off to Masamoto Lodge, by Lake Manyara in Tanzania. In the night I hear an elephant munching his way across the grass and in the morning see steaming dung outside my tent. He was very close last night. I walk to the lake to take photographs. I have the menacing snort of buffalo to my left, elephants grazing to my right, and hippos ahead. On the way back, I see some naughty baboons. Sometimes I think I like the safety of the jeep.

The next day I'm bouncing along in the back of the jeep when Roland lets out a shout. 'Eureka!'

What? Then I see it. The most beautiful milky-white giraffe. It is magnificent. We race through the undergrowth, bouncing over huge rocks to get close, but the giraffe gallops away. We are stunned. To see an albino giraffe is a very rare sight. Later we see other naturally-coloured giraffes, but they don't welcome the albino. It will be an outcast for the rest of its life.

Ngoragora Crater

Next stop, the Ngoragora Crater. This crater is the world's largest 'collapsed' volcano, formed over eight million years ago. It is over 600 metres deep and 20 kilometres in diameter. The crater is shrouded in mist and the clouds look like soft cotton-wool sliding around the mountain. The jeep slowly descends the steep muddy road. The clouds part

WHITE GIRAFFE TINY TAN SPOTS ON HIS NECK

Sitting on elephant bones in the Ngoragora crater.

A rhino and lion walk past my jeep.

and tease me with a glimpse of the land below. The plains are teeming with animals and I can't decide what to photograph first. We drive past a herd of buffalo, see rhinos in the distance and lions lazing in the sun. One male lion saunters past the jeep, not even bothering to look up. This is his territory. The pride is nearby, all curled up together, limbs entwined.

I look through the binoculars at the rhinos I saw earlier. One starts lumbering towards me, getting closer and closer. Like the lion, it just walks past the jeep, not even looking in my direction.

Roland stops by a stream and we have a picnic. It is so peaceful sitting by the jeep eating lunch. Suddenly there is a *fluff, fluff* sound of wings and a large kite bird snatches my chicken leg from my hand. I get such a fright. Later, when I climb back into the jeep, I nibble nervously on an apple, but cover it with my hand. The first day in the crater has been great.

Lions entwined around each other having a sleep.

Tanzania

After two days in the crater we drive to the Serengeti in Tanzania. Roland has hired a cook and helper, and we all squeeze into the jeep. He has decided to camp by the Ndutu Lake opposite Hugo van Lawick's camp. Hugo is a famous photographer who was married to the primologist, Jane Goodall.

I walk around to find a good place to pitch my tent. I decide the best location is next to a large tree. I'm

My tent in the Serengeti.

Wildebeest gathering for the migration.

getting used to living in a tent, but I still don't like all the creepy crawlies.

In the evening I listen to the bush radio. I sit on the jeep with my drink and watch the glorious sunset. As soon as it is dark, all the insects come out. They are attracted to the light of the hurricane lamp and dive bomb my food. I'm always picking bugs out of my dinner. Eating has become a challenge!

Going to the loo outside the tent is a bigger challenge. I go to sleep early, about 8 pm, so inevitably I wake up later and want to go to the toilet. I unzip my tent and walk as far as I'm brave enough to go in the dark. One night my pyjama pants scoop up a nest of ants. My yowling

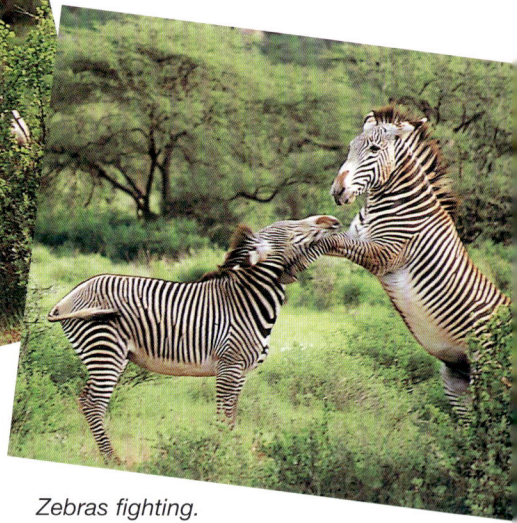

Zebras fighting.

must wake up every animal in the area. I hear a lion roar, but he is far away.

The Serengeti has hundreds of wildebeest gathering on the plains for the yearly migration. They are strange-looking animals. My guide says it looks like a committee has designed them, with a bit of every animal joined together. The migration is dangerous because the wildebeest have to clamber down the steep banks of the river to cross the raging torrents. They will risk the crocodile-infested waters to cross to the tender grass on the other side. Zebras will also walk with them and lions, waiting for their chance to hunt on the way.

Suddenly we are surrounded by the *he-haw* noise of a herd of zebras. Two zebras start fighting. They bite each other's necks, twisting and turning to kick each other, then there's a chase across the plains.

Nanyuki

An early start and a long drive back to Nanyuki to stay with Karl and Kathy. Karl has sent me some photographs of Mzee painting, and I can't wait to see them. When I arrive, Mzee flings his arms around me and gives me a huge hug.

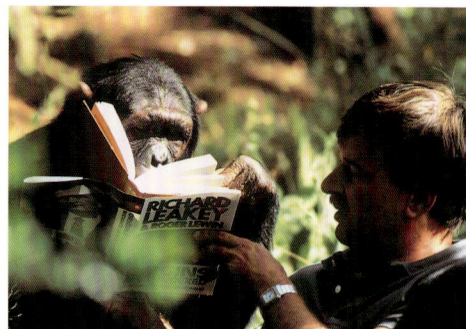

Mzee painting and reading with Karl.

He is two years older now and has become very curious. He lifts up my jumper to see what's underneath. I go upstairs to change and put a belt around my waist. When I come down again Mzee notices the belt. So he tries to fit his hairy head down the top of my jumper. I can't stop laughing.

I ask Karl and Kathy if I can go to the area where the cheetah came up to me last time I was here. They agree, and we jump into the jeep the next morning. It's only an hour's drive but I feel it's forever because I'm so impatient to see the cheetah again.

I walk with Karl to the same area and hear a loud purring. There is my cheetah. He walks up to me and I talk softly to him. I kneel down and put my hand under his throat to feel the vibration of his purring. To be so close to this magnificent animal, to touch him, is the most magic moment of my life.

Another cheetah cautiously walks up to join the first cheetah. I can see he's nervous, his hairs are standing up on his back. He comes closer. I give my camera to Karl because I want a photograph of this once-in-a-lifetime event.

The cheetahs play and romp together and I get some wonderful photographs. They will feature in the next True to Life book on cheetahs. And they are a memory I will keep forever.

A magic moment in my life, being so close to these cheetahs and watching them run free in the wild.

43

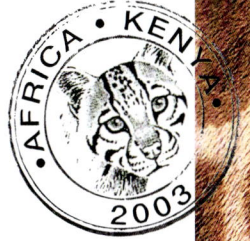

CHAPTER FIVE

The magic of Africa

I want to go to Kenya again and I start to plan my next trip. First, I research all the areas where I can get close to animals with the assistance of a good guide. I must avoid the rainy season. After the rains the grass grows very tall and the animals can hide. So I plan to go at a time when the babies are born. This is sometimes dangerous, because mothers will be very protective of their new babies, but it's great for photography.

Karl has recommended a good travel agent called Martha at Muthaiga Travel and we exchange many emails for my next trip. With great excitement I pack my bags and fly to Nairobi again. A taxi collects me at the airport and we drive to the Fairmont Hotel. Armed guards stop us outside the hotel. They look under the car with mirrors, then they inspect my luggage. Why, I ask the driver? The Israel Embassy is opposite my hotel. Police are expecting trouble, but thankfully nothing happens.

Next morning I am the only passenger on the flight to Nanyuki, so the pilot invites me to climb into the co-pilot's seat. It's great fun flying under the clouds and close to the ground, seeing herds of impala and gazelle out on the plains. Elephants lift their trunks and bellow at me

from below. I am told later that it's rather dangerous flying low because if there is a malfunction, the pilot doesn't have time to correct the plane. But we land safely.

Jason, Karl's chimp assistant, meets me and drives me to the house. After saying hello to Karl and Kathy I go up to see Mzee. Karl won't let me go into the enclosure now because Mzee is very big and strong. He wouldn't want to hurt me, but doesn't know his new strength. A chimp is much stronger than a man, so if anything happened, Karl might not be able to help me. I have to be content to be groomed between bars.

Mzee's huge black hairy hand comes out to groom my face. He softly touches my hair and gently plays with my hand. I've never been so smitten with an animal. He must feel my affection for him because he offers me his banana. A great acceptance! That night when he goes through his private entrance into Karl and Kathy's bedroom, he looks for me. He opens the curtains, looks through the keyhole and, when he can't find me, settles down to watch TV. He stays with Karl and Kathy until morning.

Karl wants to show me his latest book, *Consuming Nature*. He has spent over thirteen years taking photographs, often in dangerous situations, of the bush meat trade in the Congo. He's very disappointed with the book so I agree to re-design and produce the book again for him. It is a monumental task to undertake. First, the book is 200 pages and second, I will have to suffer the cruel photographs on my computer screen for the next few months. Some of the photographs are shocking. But this is a book to stop the slaughter of the primates and the trading of bush meat, so I want to do it.

It has been raining for a few days, but the next day the rain eases, so Jason drives me to Sweetwater, the

Mzee giving Karl a kiss.

chimp sanctuary. Ann Olivecrona, who looks after the sanctuary, has just rescued four tiny baby chimps. She will nurture them until they are ready to go to the sanctuary. They are adorable bundles of mischief. My camera bag is unzipped, my lens licked and explored. I play with them for a wonderful hour. Then we bounce and slither back through the mud in the jeep. I get out to photograph two stately giraffes. Jason calls out, 'Watch out for lions!'

I think he is joking, but round the bend is a lonely lion basking in the sun. To think I was wandering down the dirt track all alone!

Karl lets me get close to Bili today. She is a female chimp who plays with Mzee. Bili is lying down and I lie next to her. I start to groom her foot. With great concentration I examine all the hairs on her foot, occasionally looking up at her. She looks at me with her black curious eyes, and we test each other. Karl warns me to be careful because she likes to bite.

I am leaving for Intrepids Camp, so I go to say good-bye to Mzee. He waves back at me and I nearly burst into tears.

Samburu

Kathy drives me to the grassy airstrip and I fly to Samburu. This is my second time at Intrepids Camp. My tent is on a high wooden platform up in the trees, overlooking the river. The monkeys are still a nuisance and I have to keep my tent zipped up all the time. Once I forget and, in a second, a monkey and her baby are at the flap of my tent. A quick loud clap of my hands and they are gone.

My guide is called Inuid. He drives me close to a herd of elephants and stops the open jeep. Elephants are all around me and after a while I realise I'm in a rather

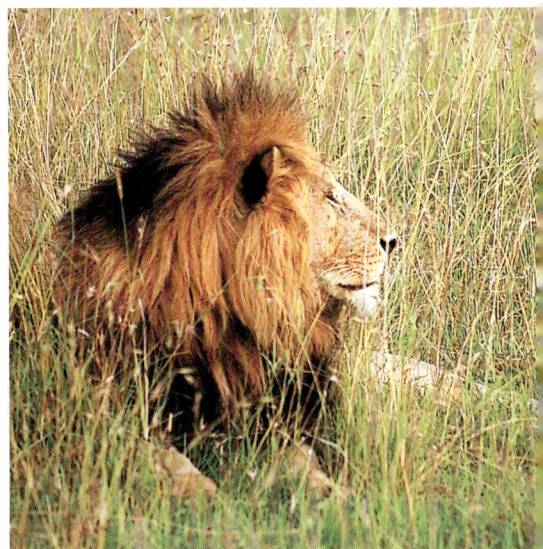

Lonely lion on the grassy plains.

Two adorable chimps at Sweetwater sanctuary.

tight 'elephant sandwich'–
one big elephant in front
and one behind. They start
tossing mud over their
bodies and I get splattered.
We wait for them to amble
away.

My tent in the trees at Sambura.

Back to my tent and a
Maasai in colourful costume jogs past. 'Jumbo', he says,
which means 'hello'. He plays the flute while I'm having
lunch. At first I think how nice it is to have music but then
I am told his music keeps the naughty monkeys away. He
has a hornbill bird as a pet.

The next day I visit Oria Douglas-Hamilton at her
new Elephant Walk Camp. She is the wife of Ian Douglas-
Hamilton, the famous elephant scientist. When she has
guests she makes a camp by hooking up tents under the
huge trees by the river. All the furniture is constructed of
branches and logs. I sit in a branch chair and it is very
comfortable.

Amboseli

Off on Air Kenya again to Amboseli. I've been told that
Tortilis Camp is closed due to a Maasai dispute, so they
have relocated me to Serena Lodge. The rooms are
adobe-style huts set in lush gardens. Some of the staff
wear traditional Maasai cloaks, with beautiful beads and
decorative head dresses. They are very handsome, their
skin like melted chocolate, some polished mahogany,
others a deep blue-black.

My first game drive is great. A herd of elephants walks
past my jeep on their way to the river. Little babies are in
the herd and they are so funny to watch, loping along,

The flute player and his hornbill bird.

playing with their food and generally getting under foot. They don't know what to do with their rubbery trunks, and swirl them around their face with a look of amazement. 'What is this curious thing on my face?' they seem to be asking.

An elephant's funny trunk action.

One newly born calf is so tiny she flops on the ground after suckling her mum. The mother gently nudges her up with her foot, then she flops down again. This is repeated many times until an 'auntie' comes to look after the calf so the mother can graze. The mother and baby calf are reunited and the mother lets out litres of urine on the baby, followed by a ton of manure. It sounds yucky, but the calf will eat the mother's manure when it's a little older to get nourishment from the straw-like remains.

With the herd all around the jeep, I started to notice the amusing 'trunk action' of the older elephants. Some rest their trunk on their tusks, others twist their trunk into a knot. Mothers, called cows, greet each other by curling their trunks around each other in an affectionate embrace.

The negative side of the game drive is that we have to stay on the dirt track, so often animals are too far away for good photography. The roads are bone-rattling rutted tracks that try to empty my mouth of fillings.

In the evening my room is like an oven and I'm glad I will be leaving in the morning. My guide, Letaloi, from Tortilis Camp, collects me and I have my first real game drive off the road. Letaloi is so huge he could wrestle a buffalo, but he's also very gentle. He's an excellent

A mother and her newly born baby.

guide and quickly finds a pride of lions.

My tent at Tortilis Camp is fabulous. I have a big comfortable bed, a space to hang my clothes, and a bathroom area. The tent has a thatched roof above the canvas and this keeps me cool in the heat of the day. When I turn back the front flaps of my tent, Mount Kilimanjaro is perfectly framed. In the morning it's soft and mauve, later in the day it's covered by cloud.

Mount Kilimanjaro is the tallest free-standing mountain in the world. It has the highest peak in Africa, 5,895 metres. Sadly, because of global warming, the snow on top has almost melted.

Playful mongoose.

Outside a parade of animals passes by – impala and bush bucks. Then I get a fright because I think I see rats rustling in the bush. But when they are close I notice their cute little faces and realise they are mongooses. They scuttle around the tent, in and out of the bush, and entertain me with their antics.

The camp has a main building at the top of the hill, which is where the restaurant is located. The owner of the camp, Stefano Cheli, asked his mother to train the chef to cook good simple Italian cuisine. The camp has a herb and vegetable garden so every day I eat freshly picked vegetables. Very healthy!

A parade of animals passes my tent.

Letaloi drives me out in the afternoon. I watch two cheetahs stalk a baby impala. They take their time, sauntering towards the impala. Slowly they part, one on each side of the baby, and pounce. The baby makes a run for it, but after a bleating cry, is silenced. The mother impala runs back, but it's too late. Her baby is gone. She trots off, turns back for one last look, then runs away.

I'm the only guest in the camp and feel a tiny bit nervous because my tent is a long way from the main

My tent at Tortilis Camp, looking out to Mount Kilimanjaro.

building. In the evening I meet Sue Heath, who is the Operation Manager and she will be in the tent next to mine. This is comforting because the African night has many spooky noises.

As I zip up my tent for the night, silhouettes of animals trot past. I can't stop smiling. My first day has been fabulous.

I ask Letaloi to drive me to the local Maasai village. When I arrive, the villagers welcome me with a traditional dance. I ask permission to photograph details of their jewellery, decorative hairstyles and vibrantly coloured clothing. They are very shy and polite and don't pressure me to buy anything. It is a nice experience.

Maasai Mara

One last game drive, then I fly to Intrepids Camp in the Maasai Mara. I have a handsome driver called Dedan. He is very knowledgeable about the animals in the area. He's spotted three lions out for the evening hunt. We wait for half an hour before the action starts.

A herd of zebra sees the lions and they give a warning bark. The male zebra waits for the herd to be

Colourful Maasai clothes and jewellery.

Mother and baby impala.

Cheetahs with a kill.

Mother cheetah teaching her cubs to hunt.

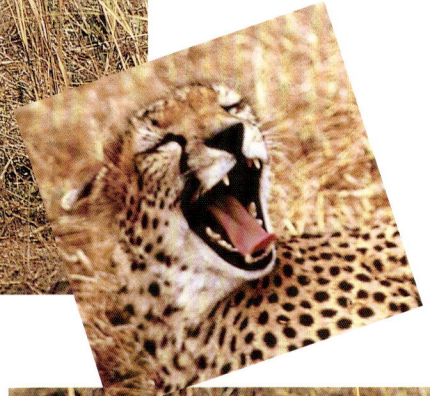

away from the lions and out of danger, then they gallop away. The lions are stalking a gazelle left out in the open, away from the herd. She's very nervous because she can't see the lions but she knows they are there. They are circling. One is so still I think I've been watching a rock until she moves. The others are coming in for the kill. They crawl slowly on their bellies. Closer and closer. It really is horrible to watch another animal being killed. But this is Africa. All animals need to feed to survive.

Next day I see a leopard up in a tree, with her kill dangling from a branch. She will feed on this for days, and she has cubs hidden close by. We drive out onto the plains and watch a mother cheetah teach her three cubs how to hunt. This is rather gruesome, but it's fascinating to watch the mother give the lesson. After they consume the baby gazelle, the cheetahs groom one another then come and flop down in the shade of my jeep. I'm in heaven, and the temptation to reach out and touch them is intense. The mother climbs onto the jeep and looks through the window. Next, she climbs onto the canvas roof, her tail is left twitching in front of my face. I can't stop grinning.

After a heavy downpour we find a pride of lions

Grooming each other after eating.

53

Grooming and playing.

and they are frolicking with their cubs. Little ones are walking over mum's head, pulling at tails, trying to climb trees and having a great time together. Usually lions are covered with flies, but after the heavy rain, these lions have no flies. They are so handsome I decide they will all feature in the next *True to Life* book.

Every night I hear a hippo outside my tent, munching his way down the river. He lets out a blood-curdling grunt that sometimes gives me strange dreams. But the great thrill is to hear the lions during the night – the wonderful throaty sound they make after a mighty roar, followed by three coughs. In the morning we find them again, and watch them in the glorious golden morning light.

Later, back at my tent, a baboon is cracking seeds and I'm tent-bound until he leaves. Bit of a nuisance, but they bite. My underwear and socks have been stolen and I'm a bit cross. But it is funny to think of the baboon with my clothes.

For five days now we have searched for the mother

Climbing a tree.

leopard and her cubs. Dedan thinks he knows where they are, so we set off early the next morning. We find them. One baby is up a tree, with legs dangling down from either side of the branch. The other is timidly walking towards me. I feel it's a great privilege to be able to get so close to one of Africa's most elusive animals. Another jeep arrives and scares the mother and babies away. We reluctantly drive off.

And now thousands of wildebeest are starting the long migration back to the Serengeti. The lions are sleeping in the sun, mother cheetah is still teaching her young, hippos are cooling off in the river, the zebras are skittish, Cape buffalo menacing, the little tails of the gazelles twitching, and the circle of nature continues.

There is something mesmerising about Africa. It is magic. I can't wait to return!

Mother leopard and her cub (above).

CHAPTER SIX

Following the elephants

I have been reading all the books written by the scientist, Cynthia Moss. She researched the elephants in the Amboseli area for over 30 years. My experience with elephants so far has been exciting and sometimes frightening, but after reading Cynthia's books I have a better understanding of elephants' behaviour. So I book my trip to Nairobi, and Tortilis Camp again, to follow the elephants. This time for another *True to Life* book.

After a long flight to Nairobi, I dump my bags at the hotel, grab my camera, jump into a car and go to meet Angela Sheldrick. Angela is the daughter of David and Daphne Sheldrick, who started an elephant orphanage in 1977. In one of our many email exchanges, Angela has said she will not allow me to go into the bush to photograph the elephants, it's too dangerous. She has suggested I visit during the public viewing time. I don't want to do that, so I have made an appointment to meet her.

I arrive at the David Sheldrick Orphanage and we have a cup of tea together. Then I meet Dame Daphne Sheldrick, Angela's wonderful mother. When I say I have travelled for 24 hours without sleep and I'm passionate

An egret rides on the back of an elephant.

The dreamy eyes of a giraffe.

about seeing the baby elephants, she agrees to let me go into the bush. She introduces me to Jacob, a Samburian warrior who found one of the orphans. Each orphaned elephant, called a calf, has its own keeper. The keeper stays with his calf all day. He sleeps with it in the stable at night and gives it milk bottles on demand, which is often. He puts a blanket on it when the weather is cold and covers the calf's delicate soft skin when the sun is too hot.

Jacob and I start walking into the bush. He has such a long stride as he is used to walking for days in the country. I'm a bit breathless trying to keep up with him. I'm also a little nervous, not knowing what to expect. It starts to rain and in minutes I have mud up to my knees. I keep sliding all over the place and grab at anything to keep from falling. I stop suddenly. A huge giraffe is looking at me from a great height. Jacob says, 'Hakuna matata,' which means, not to worry. 'All the animals are friendly when they see my green jacket, even lions.'

Lions? I'm standing in the rain with a Samburian warrior holding an umbrella, in the middle of the bush. Lions?!

I wade across a stream and on the other side are nine baby elephants. They squeal with excitement when they see us and run towards me. I have elephants all around me. Some are tiny, up to my waist, and others to my shoulder. They are very strong and I slip and slide in the mud from their playful pushing until I can hang onto a bush for support. Their trunks curl around my waist and explore my face and shoulders. It's wonderful.

One little elephant sucks her keeper's fingers, then curls her trunk seductively around his face. I put my fingers in to feel the calf's tongue and she sucks away with a look of pure contentment. The suction gets rather strong and I wonder how I'm going to remove my hand.

The rain is torrential now so I can't take any photographs. Pity, so many lovely images! It's fascinating to be so close. The elephant's ears feel like soft leather and have a tiny row of hairs, almost like a little mane. The tops of their ears fold back on their heads like tan cabbage leaves. The hairs on their trunks are very coarse and the tips of their trunks are always exploring me. Long, coarse eyelashes protect their eyes. There is a pale blue rim

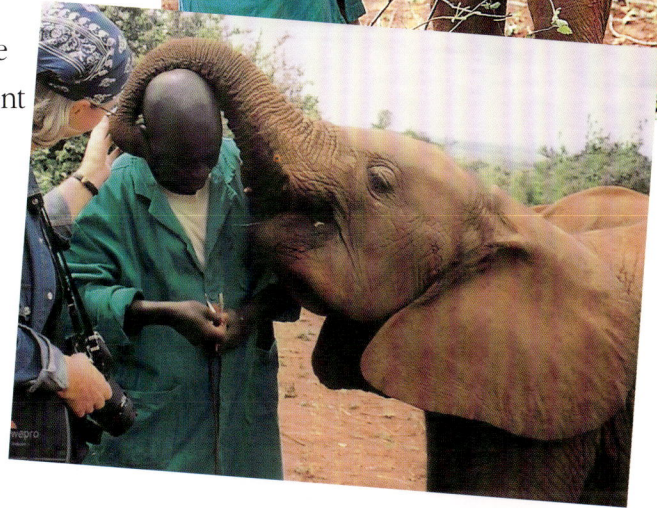

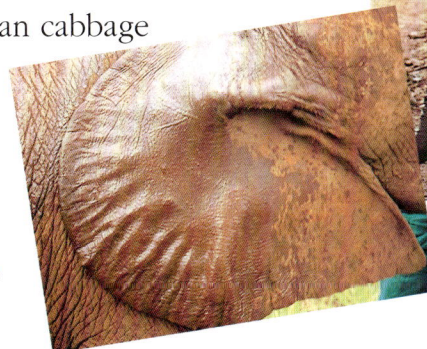

Affectionate calves and their keepers at the David Sheldrick Elephant Orphanage.

around their eyes which sometimes gives them a frightened look.

When it's time for their milk bottles we all walk back – nine elephants in single file, then their keepers, and then me. When the orphans get close to the stables they start running. My keeper's baby is impatient and starts squealing and running around in frustration, flapping his

Feeding the giraffes at Giraffe Manor.

ears, until he gets his bottle. Just like a naughty child! He finally calms down after his milk bottle and his stomach rumbles with contentment.

After the orphanage I stop at the giraffe centre. I can't resist being close to them. Their beautiful faces come up to mine, their long purple tongues quivering with anticipation, stretching longer and longer until I pop the tasty pellets I have in my hand onto their tongues. They have dreamy, beautiful eyes with long, seductive eyelashes and lips that curl back when feeding. I feed two at once and get myself into a terrible tangle of head butting. I take photos in the rain because I can't help myself.

Back to the Fairview Hotel for a well deserved sleep. Up early to get to the airport and lock myself out of my hotel room with my luggage still inside. I watch in horror as, in slow motion, the door closes and I can't stop it in

time. Panic! I knock on every door but nobody will answer at 5 am. I'm rescued by one of the hotel staff who unlocks the door so I can retrieve my bags. I make a hurried exit to the airport.

Nanyuki

I'm flying to Nanyuki again to see my friends Karl and Kathy Ammann. When I fly on small planes in Kenya I can only take one small bag weighing 15 kg. I nervously watch as my bag is weighed and it is okay. But my large handbag, which I sling across my shoulder, is very heavy and I try walking out onto the tarmac without leaning to the left with the weight.

The tiny planes are great fun. Some are four-seaters, others take up to 24 passengers. The co-pilot gives us the safety rules and after joking about the in-flight entertainment passes around a basket of sweets. After an hour we land on a grass airstrip and Kathy is there to meet me. We drive back to the house and I'm greeted by the staff and a noisy group of dogs.

Karl has just returned from Borneo and after saying hello goes to the computer to answer hundreds of emails from all over the world. When he finishes some of the more important emails he takes me to see Mzee. Karl warns me that he might 'display', which means all the hairs stand straight up on his head. But he doesn't, he comes over for a rubbery kiss. I give him three sweets and he delicately unwraps each one, pops them in his mouth and gives me the paper wrapping. He munches away on the sweets, occasionally exploring my shirt pocket for more. Then it's grooming time. He softly touches my hair, cheek, eyebrows, plays with a freckle, then puts his finger into the corner of my eyes. I can't relax completely when I know his huge

Contrast between the lush fields and the dry earth around the Maasai huts.

Acacia trees with weaver birds' nests.

The noisy hyrax.

hands will touch the corner of my eye, but he's so gentle.

My guest room is on the top floor and Kathy tells me there is a hyrax in residence. The hyrax is a small furry animal that looks like a rabbit, but has short, rounded ears. It has long claws that make a loud scratching sound in the roof. The scratching starts as soon as I climb into bed. Then the noise gets louder and louder. I think, well, I can get used to this. But then there is a moan, a whimper, then sighing sounds. I'm never going to get to sleep with this noise! Then I realise it's Rex, Karl and Kathy's Jack Russell, who's come to look after me for the night. He's very protective. Every time I'm almost asleep I hear his tippy toenails scratching across the wooden floor and see his little face looking up at me. This is repeated too many times for a peaceful night's sleep, but he's such a good 'guard dog' I don't mind.

Next morning Kathy drives through the muddy roads to Sweetwater, the chimp sanctuary, where I meet Ann Olivecrona again. She has three tiny orphaned chimps that run up to me when we arrive. I try to take photos but

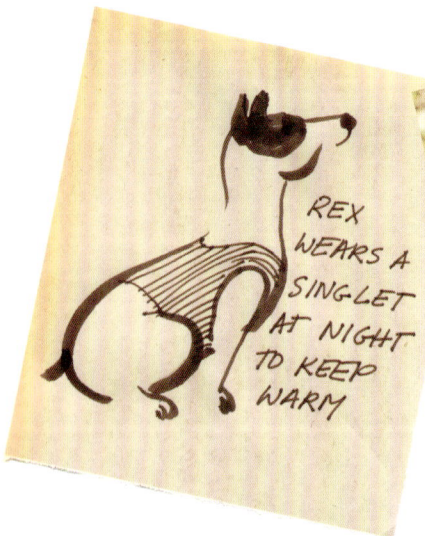

REX WEARS A SINGLET AT NIGHT TO KEEP WARM

Holding an orphaned chimp at the Sweetwater Chimp Sanctuary.

A baby elephant learning to use its trunk.

An elephant uses its ears to cool its body.

they're all over me. One takes my hand so I can go for a walk with him, another tries to bite my shoes along the way and the third hugs my leg. It's so special to have a little chimp come up and hold my hand, climb up on to my camera bag and look into my face with such trust. They are adorable.

I leave Nanyuki a day early because I want to see the baby elephants again, in good weather. Kathy has suggested a new guest house, Mucushla. I have a fabulous room with a four-poster bed, mosquito netting billowing under the fan, and a tangle of jungle outside. There is a small pool just outside my room and after a cooling swim I have lunch. I discover later I'm the only guest and it's wonderful to be pampered.

The next morning I hire a driver to take me to the orphan elephants. This time I'm lucky, the sun is out. I go to the public viewing area and watch as an ill-tempered rhino comes charging out, but a keeper calms him down. Then the baby elephants come out at a run for their milk bottles. Greedily they slurp the milk down and look at their keepers for more. Then it's play time and a lovely roll in the mud. I'm allowed to go beyond the roped-off

public area and get tangled up again with their playful pushing and exploring trunks. Angela tells me if I breathe into the end of an elephant's trunk, it will always remember me. I will never forget these baby orphans.

Maasai Mara

I fly to Little Governor's Camp at Maasai Mara. After landing I wait for a Maasai tribesman to row me across a raging muddy river in a tiny canoe. I find it frightening, and hang on to the rope with white-knuckle hands. We make it to the other side and I meet my driver. I hate the jeep as it has glass in the windows, so I request another open one. I'm also given a tent wa-a-a-y at the back of the camp, so ask to be moved close to the centre. Not a good start so far. But my new tent is great, and I'm camped on the Mara River. There are no security fences so when I want to go

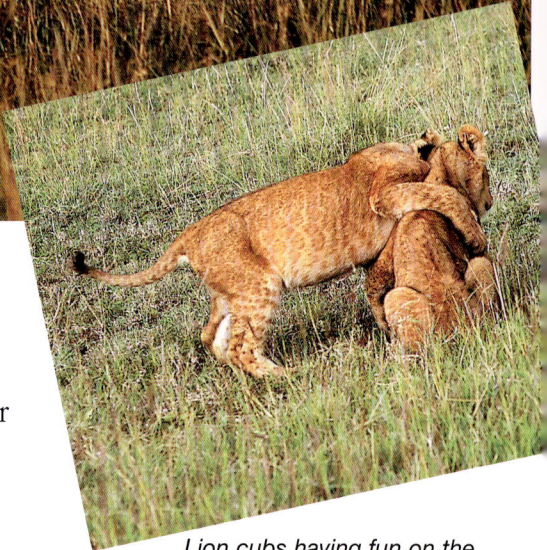

Lion cubs having fun on the plains of the Maasai Mara.

out in the evening I unzip my tent and wiggle my torch. Surprisingly, a man always appears to escort me.

Hippos come out of the river, all shiny and wet, looking like grand sculptures. They munch their way across the lawn. Now I know why the camp has such a manicured look.

I sleep with the hurricane lamp on, because I don't know how to turn it off safely. The hiss of the lamp drowns out the night noises, except the hippos. The grunting, coughing sounds are very loud and in the morning I see them outside my tent by the river.

5.30 am. My guide drives out onto the muddy tracks to the plains. For the first hour, nothing. Not one animal to be seen. I'm so disappointed! Then two handsome male lions strut into view. Next, we find the pride lolling in the grass. It's great watching the antics of the cubs – stalking, biting mum's tail, pouncing on each other. The males tolerate the cubs but occasionally bat them with their huge paws when they become a nuisance. We bounce back through the mud to breakfast. It's a shame the rains are late this year, driving in the mud is so dangerous.

After breakfast, another game drive. The guide nearly runs over a lion on the way out. She's on the track and covered by tall grass. On the way back we nearly run over her again. She hasn't moved in over two hours. I notice a large hole in her chest, smothered with flies. She must be injured and unable to move. She will not survive the night.

In the afternoon the plains are empty of animals again until we reach the plateau. Then there are hundreds of them. The topis are posing on top of the termite mounds in theatrical style, a herd of elephants on the

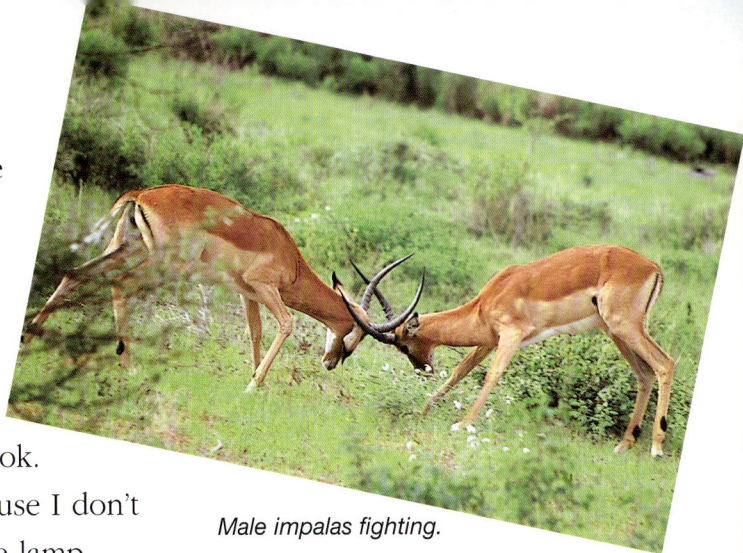

Male impalas fighting.

Bat-eared fox.

A male lion sniffing for danger.

Topis posing on termite mounds.

A hippo comes out of the water to graze.

move eats the landscape, gazelle and impala nibble on the grass.

7.30 pm and the hippos come out on cue. They look rather comical out of the water with their enormous bodies, tiny little legs and ballerina hooves. Four mounds of folded flesh hoover up the grass and the sound of munching jaws is too loud for comfort. The dining room tent is on a cement slab surrounded by succulent grass, and they're munching their way over. A spotlight keeps them at a distance, but it's not good for a relaxing meal. The night is full of the sound of lions, great throaty coughs trying to outdo the hippos' grunts. They are very close to camp.

A mother lion greets her cub.

I've mastered the lamp and sleep through the night for the first time.

Last game drive. Five minutes out of camp I see two mother lions and five cubs trotting down the road. It's still dark so we follow them, the morning light high-lighting their bodies. It's a delight to follow five bobbing baby lions. We try to overtake them. The mothers turn around, staring with cold yellow eyes, and block our path. So we patiently follow them for over an hour until they reach their destination. Then they walk into the high grass and disappear. 'Oh, no,' I groan, 'after following them for so long!' But I decide to wait and finally one mother and her cubs come out of the tall grass. Patience always pays off.

Back to the tent to pack. I have nine hippos outside my tent now. Occasionally one will lift its tonnage out of the water and leave a watermark down its body. They recline on the grassy slope. One is enormous and shoves all the others out of his way. They blend into the landscape like giant boulders.

A pride of lions with full tummies walks up the track in front of our jeep.

Amboseli

I'm waiting on the dirt airstrip ready for my next flight to Amboseli and my plane has not arrived. Another version of 'Are we there yet?' is 'Is this my plane?' The first plane won't take me but one hour and three planes later, I arrive at the Fairview Hotel.

Next morning I fly to Amboseli and my favourite camp, Tortilis. A young guide is at the landing strip to meet me. I'm disappointed it's not Letaloi, my guide from

Males eat first, then the females and last the cubs. Then they groom each other.

the last trip. I ask Sue if I can have Letaloi the next day and she says yes. This is great because Letaloi has worked with Cynthia Moss.

My 5.30 am wake-up call is tea with freshly-baked biscuits. I'm very excited to be with Letaloi again. Last night he told me about a pride of lions that looked very hungry. He is hoping they made a kill during the night, so we set off in the cold morning to find them. Letaloi searches for the cubs he saw, but they have gone. Now we have to search the whole area. Finally he says, 'Lions!' and we go charging across the dry lake.

I have an image of being stuck in the mud after all the rains, but really don't care as we race towards the pride. They have made a kill as Letaloi predicted. It's a wildebeest and the whole family is eating. Two mothers, eight cubs, one dominant male and one very old male. The pride won't share the food with the older male. Even the tiny cubs growl at him.

The cubs finally stop eating and start to play with well-chewed bones. Then a fight starts. It is ferocious, with five lions attacking each other. The noise is deafening. Letaloi sees I'm frightened and tells me it's okay, and it is. Peace is restored and a lot of grooming settles the dispute. I spend an hour taking photos and watching the pride. The mothers call their cubs and they start to walk back to the safety of the grasslands, because they are exposed out on the dry lake bed. Hyenas and vultures wait their turn to eat the leftovers.

A baby calf playing with its trunk.

A young calf takes grass from its mother's mouth.

On the way back I see two elegant cheetahs, but they are very skittish and won't let the jeep get close. Letaloi doesn't want to spook them so we drive off. After breakfast we drive out again to find the elephants.

An elephant tosses dirt over its body to protect it from insects.

Through the bushes we spot a mother with a tiny baby, just a few days old. He's wobbling along, trying to keep up with his mother. Sometimes he seems surprised by the trunk on the end of his face. He swirls it around and around, and it's a very funny sight.

When mothers give birth they leave the herd for a while and usually another elephant, called an aunty, helps the mother with the birth. After a few days they'll join up with the herd.

Letaloi sees a very large bull elephant and knows where he will cross the road so I get some great close up photographs. Letaloi's time with Cynthia Moss is so valuable because he knows which elephants are safe to get close to. I ask about Bad Bull, an elephant featured for his bad behaviour in Cynthia's book, *Elephant Memories*. Yes, Letaloi had a few close encounters in the past, but says the bull is too old now to terrorise the tourists. I'm glad!

Finally we get off the dirt track and follow a small group of mothers and young calves. I get a great photo when a baby puts its trunk into its mother's mouth to steal some grass. I know I sport a new set of wrinkles from smiling so much. I'm so happy bouncing around in the back of the jeep, covered in mud, hair covered in red dust, soaking up the beauty of the African plains.

Afternoon game drive. Letaloi drives for a long time before we see the first bull elephant. He's in musth, mating time, which means he's dangerous. As we approach he gets larger and larger, and six tonnes of elephant (the size of a double-decker bus) comes ambling towards us. I'm terrified and excited all at once. Although I have faith in Letaloi, this large bull is very close. He starts to bellow, trumpet, flap his ears, toss dirt, then he charges. We drive quickly away, then to my horror Letaloi stops the jeep. *Go, go, go*, I silently scream! The bull 'displays' by twisting his trunk in every direction, then starts to calm down. Letaloi says, 'This is Conrad, he's safe, it's only a mock charge.' Oh, he knows the elephant by name, well, I suppose I can relax! I discover I have a heartbeat again and start to take some great photographs.

Then an even bigger bull elephant comes towards the jeep. Letaloi doesn't know him, and I don't know if my heart can take another encounter, so we drive back to camp. A fabulous day. It will stay in my mind – and maybe my nightmares – forever.

Next day I have a driver called Daniel. After the

Conrad twisting his trunk in anger before charging the jeep.

excitement of yesterday, I'm relaxed about the day. Wrong! I see young elephants fighting in the swamp and we go over to investigate. The dirt road is built up from the swamp with a steep slope on either side, so there's no room for the jeep to turn around. When the group settles down, and the bull causing the fight is gone, they all continue grazing on the lush swamp grass. Another huge bull joins the group and starts walking down the dirt path.

We quickly realise that the dominant bull doesn't want us here. He menaces our jeep and we have to start backing down the road. We can't turn around, we can't go forward, and there is no exit if we go back. I'm getting very nervous. Letaloi drives up in his jeep and calls out, 'It's okay, the bull only wants to get to the bridge.' And yes, he's right again. We all take a deep breath, wait for the bull to finish his display, then he walks past us and down the track.

Elephants getting too close.

Samburu

Reluctantly I leave Tortilis and fly to Samburu, to the new Larsens Camp on the Uaso Nyiro River. My driver, Justin, is at the airstrip to collect me. He looks like a young Bill Cosby and I can't understand a word he says. The jeep won't start. It's boiling hot and there's no shade to sit in. Finally, after many coughing, choking starts, we slowly drive to the camp. Whenever Justin stops for me to take a photo, the car konks out again. I'm not happy, because this is not safe, especially from charging elephants.

But we arrive safely and the new tents at the camp are fabulous. Mine is right near the river under a huge canopy of trees.

My lunch table is set up for me by the

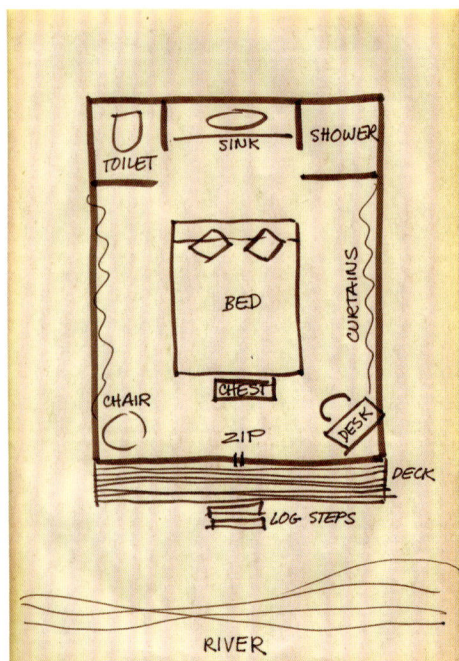

My tent at Larsens.

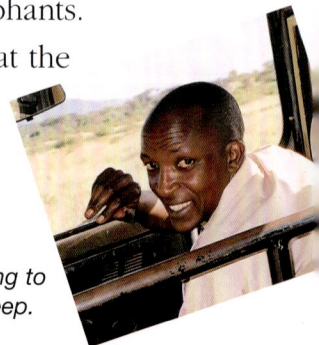

Justin trying to start the jeep.

Gerunuk standing up to eat.

river bank. I have a chef, wine waiter, server and Samburan warrior playing the flute to keep the monkeys away. I settle down to be pampered and think, this is paradise. Then across the river an elephant looks over the trees at me. It just got better!

The afternoon game drive is great. After years of trying to photograph the elusive tiny dik-dik I finally take a good photograph. Then a special sight. The elegant gerunuk is standing up on its hind legs nibbling the leaves from a tree. The gerunuk looks like a long-necked deer and always stands up to eat. Later I am very lucky and see five gerunuk, all standing up eating around the same tree.

Lunch was a novelty, but dinner is ridiculous. I realise I'm the only one at the camp. The staff put my table by a huge fire. This means they walk each course across the grass to serve me and I'm starting to feel rather self-conscious. After dinner, a guide walks me back to my tent, his torch guiding the way. I keep looking at the river, just a few metres away,

The elusive dik-dik.

A herd of elephants drinking at the river.

wondering if crocodiles come out at night.

Because I'm the only person at the camp I decide to leave the bathroom light on. I wake up in the middle of the night and it's licorice black. Silly me, I have forgotten that they would turn the generator off. I can't see my hand in front of my face. I've never experienced such dense blackness. I have to find my way to the bathroom. I feel around for the torch, can't find it and curse myself for

being stupid. Then I grope my way to the side of the tent and try to guess where the bathroom is. I spend a lot of time in the shower section and realise I've gone the wrong way. I feel my way back and finally get to my destination. Great relief, but now I have to find my way back!

The wind is howling through the tent and I can feel the inside curtains billowing around me as I try to navigate my way back to bed. The tent is interesting, with the outer

Elephants greeting each other with their trunks.

'walls' consisting of mosquito-proof netting and the inside 'walls' are curtains that can be opened or closed for privacy. In the morning I discover mosquito bites everywhere and in places I can't believe they found. First bites in two weeks and they're terribly itchy.

Morning game drive is terrific! The jeep has been fixed so we drive down to the river to wait for the elephants. They soon appear and I take hundreds of photographs of the herd having fun in the water. After drinking litres of water, they squirt water on their bodies, roll in the mud, then dust themselves with dirt. This protects them from insect bites and protects the younger ones from sunburn. I should try that for my bites!

When the herd is ready to leave, the mothers help their calves if the water is too deep for them. If the banks of the river are steep, they put their foot under the baby to help them up the muddy bank.

Helping a calf in the water.

When the herd reaches the other side of the river they start drinking again. But a crocodile has slid into the water. The vulnerable trunks in the river are quickly withdrawn with a noisy bellowing and squealing from the calves.

A lion stalks an oryx.

Another drama in the afternoon when two lions stalking an oryx are caught in the middle of a herd of elephants. One lion slowly crawls away but the other crouches down between two bushes. The matriarch, the oldest and wisest elephant, comes over to look at her. All the mothers start positioning their calves for protection, forming a circle with the calves in the middle. I think it will be dangerous with frightened elephants, but it isn't. The lion finally slinks off with its body low to the ground.

There's another unusual scene on the drive back – wild dogs chasing a hyena. The pack is hunting it down, but the hyena isn't running, it just keeps looking back, knowing its fate is decided. Driving back, we also have a close encounter with an elephant. The track has high bushes on either side and when we go around a bend a wall of elephant blocks us. We both get a fright, but thankfully the elephant just ambles off.

It has been so special to be close to the elephants. Now I have the latest information to write the next *True to Life* book and many photographs to show the life of an elephant.

Chatting to the pilot on the way back he tells me a lovely story about a pilot who flies the orphaned elephants back to Nairobi. The calves are frightened on the flight, so they put their trucks around the pilot's face and shoulders to feel safe.

Only in Africa!

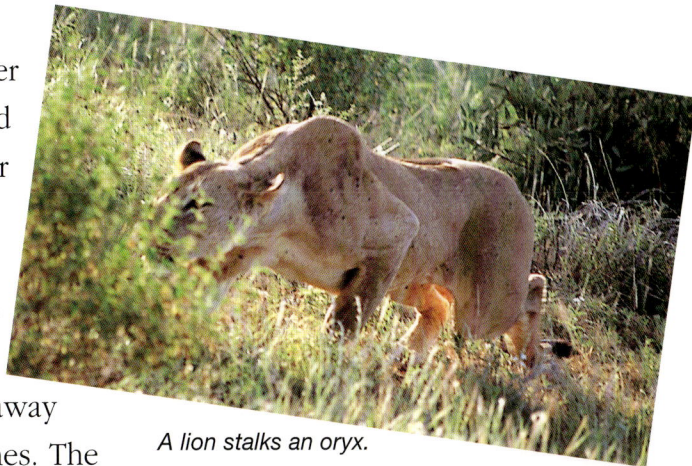

A mother protecting her calf.

CHAPTER SEVEN

Lions and luxury

I arrive in Nairobi and drive to Mucushla House. This is a ranch style house with five spacious guest rooms and wonderful attentive staff. I'm too tired to eat dinner so go to my room. A hot water bottle is tucked into my bed and I have a blissful night's sleep.

The next morning my taxi arrives to take me to Wilson Airport. We get stuck in the worst traffic jam. A 20 minute ride takes us over one hour. I start to panic because I think I will miss the plane and hope that the pilot is in the same traffic mess.

I make the plane on time and land at Samburu. Letaloi is at the airstrip to meet me, a big smile on his face. I'm so pleased to see him! We start the two hour journey to Joy's Camp in the Shaba area. The camp is named after Joy Adamson. She was a brave woman who lived in this area and reared Elsa, the famous lioness who reared all her cubs here. The camp is set among spreading acacia trees, against a backdrop of pale blue mountains.

My tent is so luxurious! Four times the size of other tents I have stayed in. I explore. The bathroom is divided from the bed area and all the amenities I need are there. The bed is gigantic, covered with soft silk pillows in exotic

colours. The curtains are inside the tent, so I can open or close them to let in the breeze. I unpack and meet Letaloi for lunch.

In the afternoon we drive out for our first adventure. I notice a terrible smell. Buffalo. Then we hear them. Hundreds are stampeding across the plains. Letaloi says something must have spooked them and we drive over to see if it is lions. He points out their pug marks in the soft earth. The lions were here recently. Then Letaloi sees a male lion and two females. Slowly we drive closer, then wait. Start the engine again, then wait. Letaloi does this because these lions are not used to people or the smell of the jeep. When we stop the third time I start to focus on the male. Through my lens I see his muscles tighten, he lets out a mighty roar...and charges. I get a terrible fright because a lion has not attacked me before. Letaloi is prepared for this and we quickly move away. When we stop and look back, the lion has settled down again

My luxurious tent under the acacia trees.

A male lion protecting his female.

with his females. I look through the lens one last time and see the black tip of his tail swishing.

On the way back to camp I see stately giraffes peering over the tops of the trees. One stands perfectly still and I take some great photographs. There is a glorious sunset as we round the corner to the camp.

I'm the only guest at the camp so I decide to have dinner in my tent. Two softly spoken men dressed in long robes come to serve me. One serves a chilled glass of

A herd of buffalo.

wine, the other my meal. It's so nice being spoilt. I have a wonderful early dinner watching the light fade and the mountains turn to dark silhouettes, keeping their secrets until the morning. I have borrowed the book *Born Free* by Joy Adamson. I snuggle into all my cushions and read until hundreds of bugs are attracted by my reading light.

The next morning Letaloi drives me to another area where all the recent rains have damaged the dirt road. It's rough negotiating the mud-bogged tracks. The jeep sinks dangerously into the squelchy mud. I see huge gouged holes where other jeeps have been trapped. This is the start of the rainy season and the landscape is very beautiful. There are tiny green shoots everywhere. A large herd of

A male elephant with three-metre long tusks.

A gerunuk pronking.

elephants is grazing on the tender shoots and as we drive away I see three massive male elephants with tusks over three metres long. They walk majestically past the jeep. A magnificent sight.

Driving back to camp I see the long-legged secretary bird prodding through the undergrowth. Then we hear a strange thumping sound. Letaloi stops the jeep. There is a coribuster bird doing a mating dance. He puffs up his front feathers and the thumping sound comes from his enlarged chest. Two females strut past. One goes up to the male and sits on the ground. After mating, the female gets up in a flurry of feathers and the male's feathers go back to normal.

I learnt a new word today. Pronking. This is when animals are very happy and jump in the air for joy. *Pronk! Pronk!* It is so funny to watch and I take some wonderful photographs.

I leave the luxury of Joy's Camp and Letaloi drives

me to meet Karl and Kathy at the border of Shaba and Samburu. Karl has been on the other side of the river taking photographs of a herd of elephants. I squeeze into the back seat of the jeep, surrounded by cases and cameras. We arrive at Nanyuki just in time for lunch. Then I go with Karl to see Mzee. Mzee grooms me then beckons me to follow him. He is a wonderful 'model' and I get some close-up photographs of his wise old face. Next, I visit Bili – the female chimp who plays with Mzee. She breaks branches and throws stones at me because I'm with Jason, her keeper. Then she goes to her platform up in the trees and sulks. It's rather funny to watch, just like a jealous woman.

Jason tells me he has recently returned from India where he bought a silver ring. After Bili saw the ring she found some silver foil and twisted it around her finger. Left hand, engagement finger. Amazing.

Next morning I fly to Wilson Airport and then on to Entebbe, Uganda, to see the chimps at Ngamba Island.

The coribuster bird.

SECRETARY BIRD
FLY-AWAY FEATHERS
FROM HEAD AND
TAIL

Mzee and his wise old face.

CHAPTER EIGHT

Cuddling chimps

In Sydney in July 2006, I have the privilege of meeting the famous primologist, Dr Jane Goodall, at Joan Pearson's home. Joan is amazing. For over six years she has been hosting charity functions for animals in need. She often has over 100 people at her home for these events. At the dinner Jane Goodall speaks about her research, saving primates and environmental issues. She is a very gentle woman and speaks softly. I can't image her alone in the jungle.

Jane also talks at a charity event at Taronga Zoo, so I go to listen to her again. After her speech, there is an auction. It's for three days at the Ngamba Chimp Sanctuary in Uganda, Africa. My bid is accepted and I prepare for my trip.

I meet Debby Cox in Sydney. She is the director of the Jane Goodall Foundation, and lives in Uganda. She says I need vaccinations before I'm allowed to be with the chimps. After seven needles my arm is very sore, but I'm safe to be with the chimps. And, more importantly, they are safe to be with me.

I am inspired to read Jane Goodall's book again, *In the Shadow of Man*. This book is a record of all her

Rambo looks into my camera.

years researching chimps in the wild. I read it with interest because I want to publish another *True to Life* book about chimps. Also, her research explains the emotions of chimps. Just like humans they have the same emotions, they can be nice or naughty! I think of Mzee and Bili.

Debby meets me at Entebbe Airport and we drive to the wharf to catch a speedboat to the island where the chimps live. For almost an hour I have a bumpy ride across Lake Victoria. This is the largest freshwater lake in Africa and known for the world's highest record of lightning strikes. I don't like lightning and thunder so I cross my fingers and hope that living in a little tent is not going be a problem.

After I arrive on the island, Debby shows me around. She arrived in Uganda in 1996 to establish the chimp sanctuary. After raising funds, the island was bought in 1997, and the chimps were finally moved onto the island in 1998. She was the Project Director until 2003, and now acts as Advisor to the Trustees of the sanctuary.

The chimps are being fed in their night enclosures so I toss my bag into my tent and go up to watch. The light is too dim to take photographs, but I do try taking one of all the chimps with their long arms sticking through the bars holding their bowls. One little orphan has the most adorable face, and I can't wait to take a photograph of him when the light is suitable.

The chimps are very noisy during feeding time. They scream and chase each other around their night enclosure. The carers give them cabbage and a porridge mixture made of millet flour. After eating, the chimps climb into their 'nests' for the night. These are made of hessian and sometimes the chimps put branches and leaves inside.

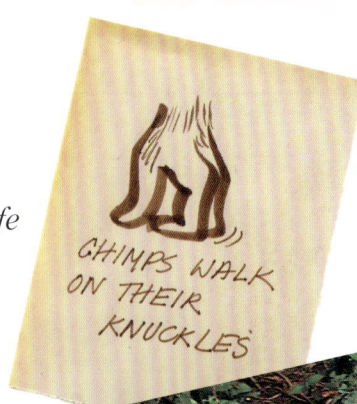

CHIMPS WALK ON THEIR KNUCKLES

Chimps walking back from the forest at feeding time.

My tent is on a platform and there are two beds inside. The sides of the tent can be unzipped to let a breeze through. At the back of the tent is a wash basin, shower unit, and a chemical toilet. (This toilet should only be used at night because it has to be emptied each morning.) When I want a shower I ask the staff to bring hot water. They tip it into a bag outside my tent and, inside, I pull a string for the water to come down. It's great fun.

I meet Debby in the mess tent and we have a superb dinner. I can't believe the cook prepared such a fabulous meal from just a tiny kitchen at the back of the tent. We discuss the next morning's walk. Debby says I must not put anything in my pockets or the chimps will take it. My small camera is allowed but needs to be hidden, and no glasses. I say I need them to take photographs, so I will have to find a way to tie them securely.

My wake-up call is 6 am and a cup of tea is left outside the tent. Now, to get ready. First, empty all my pockets. Second, tie my glasses down. Third, hide camera. Fourth, put on large green overalls to stop my clothes getting dirty. Fifth, wait for the chimps to enter the jungle.

The chimps are approaching through a security tunnel. When they emerge, a fight starts. I'm frozen to the spot. It's very frightening. Three chimps are screaming, chasing each other, baring their sharp teeth, hairs standing on end, then – it's all over. They groom one another and peace is restored. My heartbeat takes a while to return to normal. I look over at Debby and she's smiling, telling me there is no need for concern.

I start walking behind Debby and the chimp carer, called Robert. The path is very muddy and slippery and I struggle through the undergrowth. Suddenly I feel a heavy

Jane Goodall and Charlie.

My tent and the shower bucket outside on the pole.

weight on my shoulders and realise that a chimp has climbed onto my back. He wants a ride. I would love to carry him but he is too heavy. I stagger around for a while, then reluctantly ask Robert to take him off. The chimp sulks.

We come to a clearing and settle on a large log. The chimps go off to play. They swing from the vines and branches and often come tumbling down with a loud crash when the branch breaks. One chimp is concentrating on untying Debby's shoelaces. Another comes and sits next to me so I can groom her. I run my fingers through her coarse hair, looking for insects, touch her soft rubbery pink ears, then tickle her. She wriggles and giggles and we all laugh. She turns around and holds my hand, then pretends to start grooming me. But she is being naughty. She has seen my camera and knows where it is hidden and she wants it. The game starts.

Chimps are very intelligent and they are very good with tools, so it doesn't take her long to unzip my camera jacket. I quickly move away and stand behind a tree. In a second a chimp runs up the tree, grabs my scarf and has my glasses. My reflexes are good and I grab the end of my glasses. Robert says a stern word and the chimp returns my glasses to me.

Debby has her shoelaces completely undone now and she distracts the chimp by starting to groom it. The chimp in turn grooms Debby. It's a wonderful sight. Debby has her head down and the chimp, with great concentration, is going through her hair.

Debby had her early training as a veterinary nurse, then worked at Taronga Zoo in Sydney. She has a great knowledge of chimps and has worked with the orphans

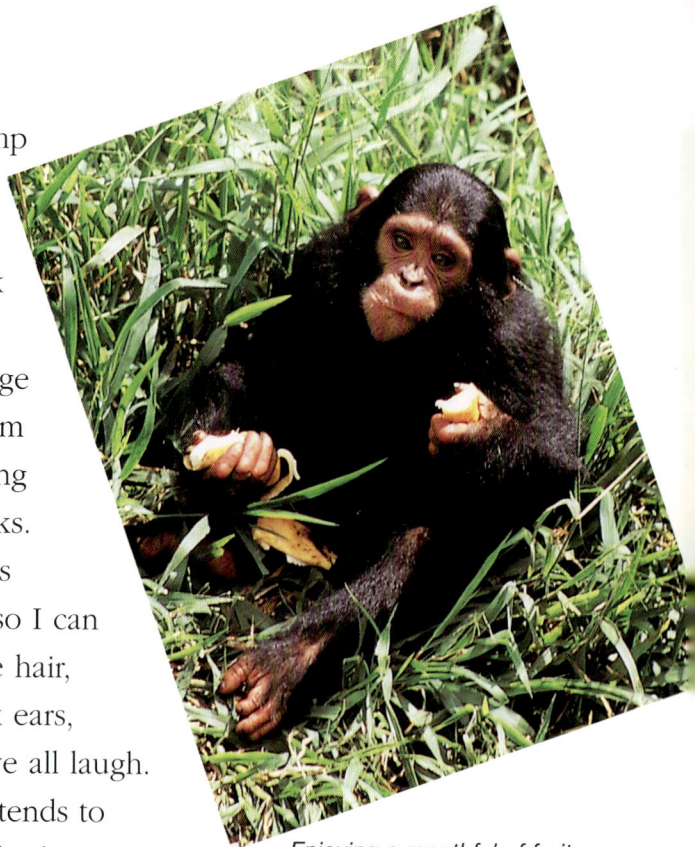

Enjoying a mouthful of fruit.

Collecting fruit.

Chimps groom each other.

for ten years. She tells me about the dominant male in the group, which female chimp adopted an orphan baby when brought into the reserve, and all the chimps' personalities. Some are very gentle in nature, others rambunctious. She also knows them all by name.

Back to the mess tent for a big breakfast then I get my film ready for the 11 am feeding time. I go to a platform so I can look down on the chimps. They start to come out of the jungle. They walk on their front knuckles, some stand up to get a better view, and others sit and wait, making soft hooting sounds. One agile chimp scampers up a huge tree. He sits in the leafy branches for a while, but coming down is not so easy.

The dominant chimps create chaos by starting fights, chasing each other and doing somersaults until the carers arrive. This time they are fed a wonderful assortment of fruits. One chimp grabs a handful of bananas and stands up so he can carry them all. Another puts so much in his mouth his cheeks look as if they will burst. Peace is

A chimp grooms its carer's hand.

restored after feeding. They reassure each other with grooming, patting each other on the head, cuddling, and embracing. They are very social and need each other's companionship.

As I walk back to my tent after dinner the sunset is glorious. Lights are bobbing on the water from hundreds of fishing boats. A tranquil scene – but not for long. I wake at 2 am to the crash of thunder. Lightning is flashing across the sky. The tent starts to sway violently and I think I am going to be swept away. I am very frightened. So are the chimps, they are all screaming. The wind gets stronger, the storm is raging all around me. I cover my camera and film with plastic. I dress and pack. If the tent is blown away I want my possessions safe. Three hours later the storm starts to subside. I crawl back into bed exhausted.

Another walk with the chimps in the morning, but this time I have a different keeper to protect me from the camera snatcher and glasses thief. It's a lovely morning after such a terrible night. We sit and watch the chimps play.

I leave the next morning to meet Debby at the Jane Goodall Institute. We go to the quarantine section to see three little orphans who have been rescued. One is tiny and is drinking from a milk bottle with a rubber teat, just like a human baby. Another is nervously sitting in the corner, the third is very active. He loves to swing from ropes, twirling around – and then he comes up for a kiss. I have my camera in my lap and he comes to look at his reflection in the lens. Next, he sits on my shoulder and I can feel his tiny fingers going through my hair, then he softly nibbles my ear. It is wonderful. His name is Rambo.

Debby and her team do a great job caring for these

Chimps love playing together.

little orphans. A carer stays with them 24 hours a day, giving them confidence, comfort, and teaching them how to adapt. Then they will join the chimps on the island. Hopefully a surrogate mother will adopt a baby and they will be accepted into the group.

Sadly I have to leave. A little face looks up at me with such trust. My heart melts. This little chimp will be in the next *True to Life* book.

It takes three days to fly back to Sydney. First, I go to Entebbe Airport at 4 am to see if I can get on a flight, as I am only waitlisted. Thankfully I get a seat and arrive at Nairobi with five hours to fill until the next flight. Do I have time to brave the terrible traffic and see the orphan elephants again? Watch them play and touch their soft rubbery trunks? It's raining, so that's not a good idea. But I might have time to feed the giraffes? No, I can't risk the traffic jams.

I do the sensible thing and wait at a hotel until it's time for my flight to Johannesburg. I stay overnight in the airport hotel then fly out the next morning to Sydney.

When the flight takes off I say goodbye to Africa. I think of all the animals I have seen. What a privilege it has been to touch a wild animal. To be close to endangered animals. To look into the eyes of a primate and be gently groomed.

I have been so lucky!

A carer comforts an orphan chimp.

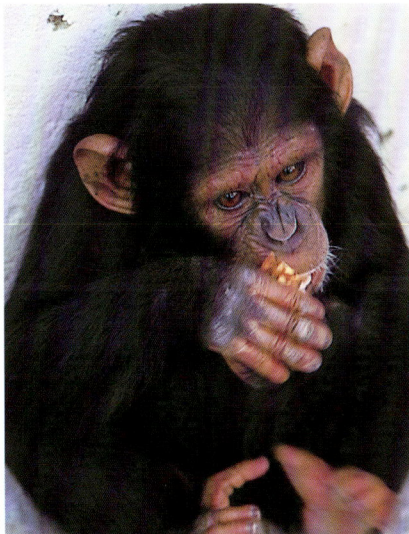

A little orphan, all hands and feet.

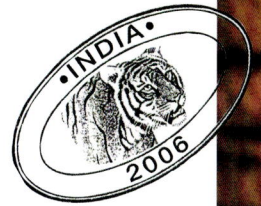

CHAPTER NINE

Tigers and Tara

I've been researching tigers for the next *True to Life* book. It is going to be a challenge finding a tiger to photograph in the wild. After many emails I am told Ranthambhore National Park, in Rajasthan, is a good place to start. So I fly to India.

I'm staying at an old hunting lodge in Ranthambhore park. It's 5 am and freezing. I'm trying to fit jeans over my woollen tights. Next I pull on my thick socks, two sweaters, a waterproof jacket and a woolly hat. Last, my woollen gloves with holes for the fingers, so I can use my camera.

My guide, Manohar Singh, says only 28 tigers were recorded in Ranthambhore Park in 1995. Fewer than ten roam the park now. How sad! Poachers are still killing tigers for their magnificent skins. And in China they are still grinding up their bones for medicine. Manohar has been at Ranthambhore for 20 years, so I'm in very good hands.

On the first morning I don't see a tiger, but the spotted and Sambar deer keep me busy taking photographs. The morning light is beautiful, a pale pink palette reflecting the old ruins of the fort and the Jogi Mahal Hunting Lodge, by the lake. I think I will see a lot of birdlife around the

lake but there's only one cheeky bird who wants to perch on the end of my camera.

In the afternoon I search the ground for the imprint of the tiger's paw, called a pug mark. The pug marks are everywhere, but no tiger. Suddenly Manohar stops the jeep. There are tiger's claw marks down the bark of a tree. I can smell his scent marking (a spray of urine) but no tiger. In the silence my heartbeat sounds loud and matches the rhythm of the jeep's clock. We wait, but still no tiger.

Another day searching for the elusive tiger without success. I'm so disappointed.

My journey in search of a tiger.

Golden light at Ranthambhore Park.

I decide to have a break from tiger searching and go to the magnificent Taj Mahal, in Agra, a long drive from Ranthambhore. The roads are congested with cows, camels, goats, and people. All drivers constantly have their hand on the horn, adding to the chaos. In contrast to the noise, the scenery is so beautiful, with acres of yellow mustard flowers in the fields. The mud huts have decorative art around the doorways. The women, dressed in colourful saris, sweep their dirt floors. Some of the people are very poor but the women have a gracious pride in the way they walk, their glorious coloured saris billowing in the breeze. They carry heavy pots on their heads and often huge bundles of wood. The men sit on their haunches in the shade, smoking.

Spotted deer in the forest.

Built in 1680 by Emperor Shan Jahan for his favourite wife, the Taj Mahal is considered one of the great wonders. It is also one of the most photographed buildings in the world, so it's a challenge for me to try to do something different. I go very early in the morning and watch it slowly come into focus through the morning mist. It's truly a beautiful sight. Later in the day I take hundreds of photographs in the glow of the afternoon light.

Back on the road again to the Madhar National Park, Shivpuri, where I hope to get permission to photograph nine tigers. The tigers are in a large enclosure surrounded

by two wire fences, and an old man is their keeper. I'm allowed to go behind the first fence to take photographs through the wire. This upsets one tiger and he lunges at me. I'm frightened speechless. I have to creep up again to take my close-ups.

Large chunks of meat are delivered and it's fascinating to watch the tiger's huge teeth rip into the flesh and grind away on the bones. I see a goat tethered a short distance away and realise his fate. In the afternoon a park ranger and his team arrive and I am told to leave. They also want extra money for me to come back tomorrow to photograph. The frail old man who is the tigers' keeper just shrugs.

On the last day there is a sign saying 'Closed', but thankfully the enclosure is open and the ranger is not there demanding more money. All the young tigers are let out to play, and it's great taking photographs of them chasing each other. They race up and down with endless energy, stalking, scent marking and finally settling down to groom one another. One tiger gives a tree a huge hug after he has sprayed it.

On the road again and a flat tyre. While I wait for help a crowd starts to appear all around me. They stand and stare. The same thing happens later when I wait for the train. It is not at all threatening, they are just curious about my blonde hair. When the train arrives there is a terrible push and shove to get on. I have booked a bunk in the first class section but that makes no difference to the noisy family sitting in my section. As it is a long journey and I have to sleep, I ask them to leave.

An elegant sheik enters the compartment and asks permission to sit down. He is splendid. I watch him

Tigers eating, grooming and stalking.

96

take off his turban and carefully place it on the seat. His hair is very long and it is twisted around his head many times. In the morning, when he dons his turban again, he tucks in his hair with a tool that looks like a long knitting needle with a hook on the end. When the sheik departs he is met at the station by an entourage of twelve men. He must be important.

The four hour jeep trip to Kipling Camp in the Kanha National Park is very rough and I'm exhausted when I arrive. I'm also disappointed with the rustic accommodation. My hut is a structure of wood with mud walls and a thatched roof. I look up to the roof and see the sky peeping back. I hope it doesn't rain.

It does.

The mornings are so cold I decide to sleep in some of my clothes with the outer layers in between my blankets. If I don't, my clothes get wet from the leaking roof and the morning dew. I move to another hut where only the shower unit leaks. The novelty of having a hot shower with cold rain is not amusing.

But all that is forgotten when I climb onto Tara. She is a beautiful, gentle elephant made famous by the book, *Travels on my Elephant,* by Mark Shand. Mark wrote about his adventures in India, travelling on Tara. When the journey was over, he gave Tara to Anne and Bob Wright at Kipling Camp.

The great thrill is to go out alone with Tara and the mahout early in the morning. The mahout is the elephant's keeper. He sits behind the elephant's ears and gently nudges him with his foot to give directions. I try sitting behind the mahout, instead of sitting sideways, but I can't get comfortable.

Tiger scent-marking a tree.

Tara leaves me on a large rock so I can have my breakfast of tea and a boiled egg. She forages for tender green leaves. She lets me get very close to her when she is eating. It is so exciting to photograph inside her huge pink mouth. She always seems to be smiling.

When she has finished eating, I climb back on to her to head down to the river. Now this is not easy. Tara kneels down and I climb onto her bent leg, hold her tail, and scramble up her rump.

Tara loves being scrubbed with large smooth stones, then she goes into the deep part of the river to swim. The only thing I can see of her is the tip of her trunk looking like a periscope. On the riverbank she dries off, then I climb back on.

A pack of wild dogs starts to follow us and Tara is spooked. She starts trumpeting, ears rigid, and backs away from them. It's so rare to see wild dogs in this part of India that I try to take a photograph. It's very difficult to focus my camera with Tara running from the wild dogs.

My tiger search has come to a halt because it's raining again. The roads are too muddy to go into the park. This is very frustrating. One the third day, the rains have cleared and I'm allowed in. I see large pug marks. Somewhere there is a tiger.

The afternoon is magic! My guide says he heard a tiger's roar in the morning and vultures were circling which means a recent kill. Then I see her. A magnificent tiger walks out of the dense forest. It is amazing. My

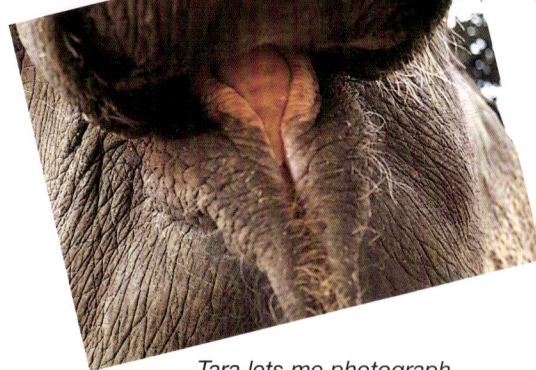

Tara lets me photograph inside her mouth.

A magnificent tiger walking out of the forest.

guide is not allowed to drive off the dirt road so I hope the tiger will walk towards me. She does. She is breathtakingly beautiful. I start clicking my camera a frame a second, I'm holding my breath at the same time. She walks closer and closer. I am purple in the face and realise I need to breathe. Many rolls of film later, I am so happy.

The tiger has recently given birth and her cubs are hiding in the jungle. When she pads purposefully back into the jungle she lets out a mighty roar. Then another. Fourteen roars later the jungle is silent. What a dramatic exit! I ask the driver if this always happens? He says this is the first time he has heard it.

It has been such a privilege to be here, worth all the months of obtaining permits and permissions and daily frustrations.

I have a long drive to Nageur with a driver who is a maniac. He overtakes on hills, around bends, and after

A wild dog following us.

Mother and baby rhino with their 'coat of armour' folds.

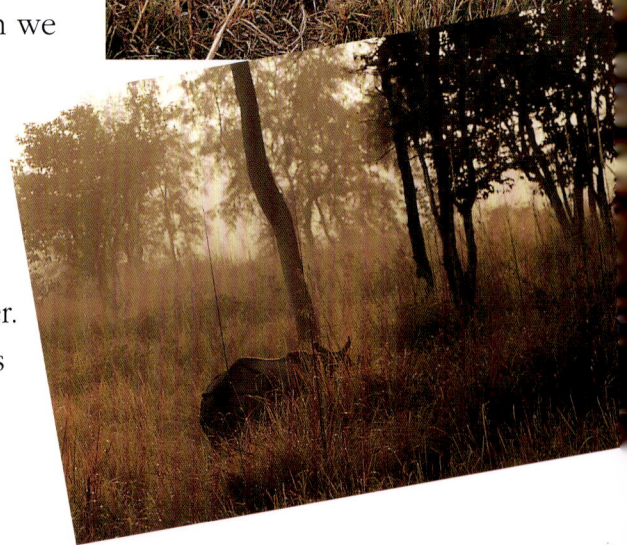

five hours I don't think I'm going to survive. But I do. I get to the airport on time and fly to Kathmandu, Nepal.

At Kathmandu I catch a taxi to Dwarika House. The hotel has been lovingly restored with exquisite carvings, huge handsome doors, and beautiful doorknobs. This is an elegant oasis in the middle of a chaotic city. I have a long, luxurious shower.

I decide to explore the city with a friend and aim for the Hindu temple I can see in the distance. When we get close I see a funeral procession. Two bodies are prepared for burial by the water. The bodies are set alight but, strangely, there is no smell.

Next day I drive to Tiger Tops. I have an elephant ride in the afternoon. The grass is over ten metres high so it will be a miracle if I ever see a tiger. But I see a mother rhino and her baby. Indian rhinos have thick folded skin that looks different from the

African elephant. They set off at a trot and I follow. Soon they are lost in the high grass.

I go for a walk with a guide along a trail and I wonder what will happen if we see a tiger or rhino. I'm told to stand very still if that happens. But nothing is going to happen because the villagers have come to burn down the grass. They are allowed to do this once a year. There is no point staying now, all the animals will run from the flames. I'm very cross I wasn't told about the fires because this has been a wasted journey. When I leave, the flames are over five metres high and I just catch a glimpse of a rhino's rump disappearing into the grass.

I travel on an elephant, cross a river by boat, climb into a jeep, and lastly a van. Another gruelling seven hours to Karnali to stay at Karnali Lodge. My room has a packed dirt floor, ethnic decorative patterns painted around the wall, and the joy of a heater.

I meet my mahout and climb onto my elephant. It's amazing riding an elephant in the jungle because the elephant makes no sound. Its huge padded feet cushion the sound. The jungle is exotic. I notice that all the vines curling around the tree trunks all curl in the same direction.

Through the morning mist I see the first pug marks. We track, wait, circle around, then hear the alarm calls of the monkeys. My heart is in overdrive. Then the mahout calls, 'Tiger, tiger!' My elephant starts screaming and bellowing and runs through the thick bushes. All I see is the tiger's tail disappearing into the jungle. But it is very exciting. My elephant finally calms down and we lumber home.

Another morning of mist, pug marks, but no tigers. The trip has been frustrating at times but it has been a great adventure and I have seen my first tiger in the wild.

Beautiful carvings at Dwarika House.

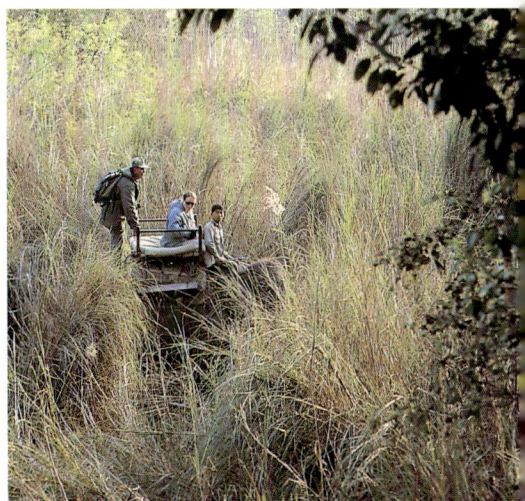
My elephant is almost hidden in the tall grass.

CHAPTER TEN

Playing with pandas

About twelve years ago I was invited to Wolong, in China, to photograph pandas at the Wolong Research Centre. I went with a small group of journalists and a cameraman from a television network. We met our guide at the centre and he walked with us to an area where a panda had been released from his enclosure. The panda was given some succulent bamboo leaves and I had the opportunity to get close to him. It was very special to touch one of the world's most endangered animals.

I could only stay for two days and asked permission to go back to photograph the panda again before I left. When I arrived at the panda's enclosure, they would not allow the panda to be released into the forest. I was very disappointed but stayed to take some photographs anyway.

A group of Chinese officials arrived. One man kept standing too close to the panda's enclosure, even though the panda's keeper told him – three times! – that it was dangerous to stand so close. The official didn't take any notice of the keeper, and the panda, who was a little bored, suddenly caught the man by his jacket and pinned him onto the bars. The man was very frightened and didn't

know what to do. My friend Jon rescued the man by pulling his jacket off and the official fell to the ground. The panda took the jacket and played with it, tossing it in the air and having great fun. The cameraman in our group filmed the event and it was shown all around the world. The man was in the wrong – the panda just wanted something to play with.

After twelve years, Wolong now has a successful breeding program. Sixteen baby pandas were born in 2005 – a world record. When I see a photograph of the tiny panda cubs, looking like cute bundles of black-and-white fluff, I decide I have to see them. I start to plan my trip, but it isn't easy. I'm not part of a group. Nobody will take a single woman, and I haven't registered as a volunteer. A volunteer is someone who will be with the pandas each day. This means cleaning up a lot of panda poo, the pandas' enclosure, and gathering bamboo for the pandas to eat. Finally the Oriental Group travel

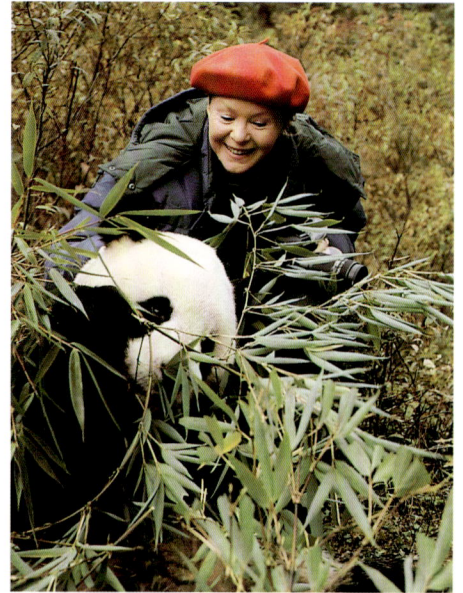

My first encounter with a panda at the Wolong Research Centre.

Areas where pandas can still be found.

company agrees to have a driver and translator meet me at Chengdu airport, the closest airport to Wolong.

I fly to Hong Kong, stay overnight with a friend, then fly to Chengdu early the next morning. I meet my translator and driver at the airport and we start our journey to Wolong Research Centre. The pollution is terrible. The whole city is covered in a thick cloud of smog. It stings my eyes and I can taste it. Ugh! I'm amazed to see an old Chinese woman cleaning the side of the road, cars whizzing past her.

Nobody takes any notice of traffic rules. A young woman (who should know better) and an old man (who is lucky to survive) start pedalling their bikes across a four-lane highway at the precise moment the lights turn green for the cars. They pedal straight in front of our car, almost in slow motion. My driver swerves, as do all the other cars. Nobody honks their horn. Everyone survives.

We leave the city and the smog and start our ascent up the mountains. New highways have been built since my last visit. Some are suspended over chasms, with steep drops below. We travel through unfinished tunnels that go straight into the mountains. One is rather scary because the tunnel has no lights. Going into a black hole is bad enough, but bouncing on uneven ground in the dark is nerve-racking. Water is dripping from the ceiling. I can't wait to get out into the light.

We leave the new highway and start climbing up another steep mountain. Some of the road has fallen away and rocks are scattered from landslides. The driver tries to pass other cars on the narrow road, but it's impossible. This is not fun. I try to take in the beauty of the mountains but I'm so nervous I can't admire the view. When the

The dramatic Wolong mountains.

A farmer with his corn harvest.

I was entertained every day by these playful pandas.

driver has to stop, I notice cabbages growing everywhere. In every space between rocks and boulders there is a cabbage. I wonder how they can grow in all the dust.

We follow a big truck grinding its way up the mountain. The driver stops and dumps huge rocks on the side of the road. All the villagers come out and start breaking up the rocks. Men and women working side by side. The young men are nimbly building a bamboo structure to support the road. This will later be filled in with the rocks, then cement will be poured into the hole for support. I try not to look at the sheer drop and the raging river below.

Finally I arrive at my hotel at the Wolong Research Centre and I'm a bit shaky as I step out of the car. The staff are very friendly and I nod and smile, trying to communicate. I'm suddenly hungry and go down to the dining room for an early dinner. I order spicy Sichuan eggplant and rice. When it arrives, it is enough for ten people. I see the bill. It's only $2. I can't possibly eat it all so I invite an American woman to join me. She tells me she's come here as a volunteer, and so far, it is very strenuous work. She says the most difficult job is carrying

the bamboo on her wheelbarrow because it's so heavy.

I go back to my room and try to boil water. The cord on the electric jug is too short to reach the wall so I have to hold the jug up in the air to boil it. This is rather dangerous so I ask for another jug. To my delight there's an electric blanket on the bed so I have a good night's sleep.

I wake to hear rain. Oh no. After a quick Chinese breakfast (boiled egg, soft roll and tea) my translator and I walk down to the pandas. I quickly discover she knows nothing about pandas and the keepers grunt and walk away. I'm disappointed because I would like to ask questions and get the latest information about the pandas.

But it's a great thrill to see the baby pandas. They are let out of their night pens at 8.30 am and make a wobbly run for their swings and play-structures. One panda has a favourite tree stump and he spends a lot of time contorting himself into different positions until he is comfortable. When he settles down, another panda climbs the tree and tries to push him off. This is very funny to watch, and for the hour I can't stop smiling. Pandas are the most adorable, cute, rambunctious animals on earth. The rain lightens to a

Trying to keep my plastic gown
on while pandas are pulling it off.

drizzle and I keep taking photographs under my umbrella.

For a 'donation' of $200 I can go into the pandas' area. I have to wash my hands, put on a plastic surgical gown, and cover my shoes with plastic. This is to protect the pandas from any germs I might have on my clothes or shoes. When I walk into the enclosure the pandas run over to me. One takes a firm grip on my leg and won't let go. Some start pulling at my gown. I try to take some shots, especially of their faces, because they look as if they're laughing at me. Then they all start pulling off my gown and I can't take any photos at all with the tangle of plastic around me. I know I'm supposed to keep my gown on but how can I with pandas playfully pulling it off? I try to drag myself along with a panda still attached to my left leg and discover how heavy he is.

To be so close to these adorable bundles, to touch their thick soft fur, it's wonderful. Ten minutes are suddenly up and I'm asked to leave. Reluctantly I go outside. I examine my leg to find I've been scratched from knee to

ankle. I don't really care, some antiseptic will take care of that after my shower. But there is no hot water. The room girl comes up to turn the taps on, but only freezing water comes out. Well, that will have to do for now.

In the afternoon I walk over to the adult giant pandas. These pandas have a large, natural area where they can roam, and the keepers feed them until they are ready to be released up the mountain into the wild. I count about twelve adult pandas and spend hours taking photographs. After eating, they sleep, so I keep circling the area waiting for them to wake up. One curls up into a huge ball to sleep, others just nod off whenever they stop eating.

Outside the baby pandas' enclosure again, I'm entertained by their antics for a second time. They are so funny, tumbling over each other, doing the most amazing trapeze contortions, then *plop*, they fall on the ground. One has become Ping-Ping the panda, the 'star'

Pandas sit or lie down to eat, then sleep, often curling up in a ball for warmth.

Pandas love playing together.

of my next *True to Life* book.

Back at the hotel reception I draw a figure having a shower and we try the hot water again. At 8 pm it is warm but the water is brown and dirt spurts out, and I decide I will be dirtier after the shower than before. I'm told that hot water will come on at 6 am and the dirt is from the rain. Tomorrow, no rain, no dirt! None of this makes any sense but I look forward to a shower in the morning.

The next morning I decide to leave in the afternoon instead of the following morning because I'm worried about the hazardous journey down the mountain and

Some of the twin pandas born in 2005.

getting to the airport on time. After a lot of negotiating with my driver, we leave after lunch. The traffic is light which is good because the driver is watching a video screen mounted on the dashboard of his car! We arrive safely in Chengdu and I check into a hotel and have a long shower followed by a bubble bath.

The next day I hear the bridge we crossed yesterday afternoon collapsed not long after we drove over it. I was shocked when I heard that – we could have plummeted down the side of the mountain. The American woman was stranded at Wolong but she bravely walked over a temporary bridge and was met on the other side. She was driven safely to Chengdu.

Before my flight there is time to visit the Chengdu Panda Reserve. The sun is out, there's no pollution and I spend an hour taking photographs in better conditions.

I fly back to Hong Kong and go straight to the lab to process my film. This is always a nervous but exciting time waiting for the results. Was I in focus? Is the colour going to be good under the rainy conditions? But the film is great and I can't wait to start writing the story. I spend three days catching up with friends then fly back to Sydney.

The day after I arrive back, I'm asked to talk to students at a local school. I show some of my favourite photographs and we discuss endangered animals. At the end of the show I say, 'Wouldn't it be sad if endangered animals disappeared from earth – the clever primates, the handsome lions and tigers, the gentle elephants. It would be very sad. So we must all do whatever we can to protect our environment and all the animals on earth.'

I hope we all do.

Pandas are very good climbers.

I would like to thank Karl and Kathy Ammann for their help and hospitality on my adventures in Africa. To Mzee who let me discover the intelligence of primates and to Moto who allowed me to get close to cheetahs. Through them I discovered the magic of Africa.

Published by ABC Books for the
AUSTRALIAN BROADCASTING CORPORATION
GPO Box 9994 Sydney NSW 2001

Text copyright © Jan Latta 2007
Photographs copyright © Jan Latta 2007
Illustrations copyright © Jan Latta 2007
Maps and calligraphy © Pat Latta 2007

First published September 2007

ISBN 978 0 7333 2040 8

Designed and typeset by Jan Latta
Set in 12.4/18 pt Garamond
Colour reproduction by Graphic Print Group, Adelaide
Printed in Hong Kong, China by Quality Printing

5 4 3 2 1

Photography credits:
Front cover: Debby Cox, Karl Ammann,
Kathy Ammann, Jon Resnick.
Also thanks to Karl Ammann for permission
to reproduce photographs on pages 20, 42,
87 and Jon Resnick for gorilla photographs
on pages 22 to 27.

All other photographs by Jan Latta.